PRAISE FOR
The Essential Rules of Love

"How much easier would marriage be with a manual? What if you could learn the rules from an attorney who's 'been there and done that?' *The Essential Rules of Love* is such a resource. Author Phil Russotti brings together his story as both a memoir and a manual that will most definitely impact your marriage.

"*The Essential Rules of Love* are not boring legalese but rather boil down to valuable 'Dos and Don'ts' that we all need to be reminded of. Ultimately an extraordinary marriage comes down to being intentional and taking action. This book, these *Essential Rules of Love*, will equip you to do just that."

—**ALISA DILORENZO,** Author of the Best Seller *The 6 Pillars of Intimacy*, Co-Founder of ONE Extraordinary Marriage

"When the love of his life died and he was beside himself with grief, Philip Russotti was thrown a lifeline by an insightful therapist: 'Do you think that, with all your life experience, you might have some wisdom to pass on to your grandchildren about how life should be lived?' It was not an empty platitude about time healing but a challenge that sent Philip down an arduous path of research and writing. As a successful trial attorney, he approached the challenge with the same rigor he brought to his professional work. What is love? What makes a relationship work? What do psychologists say? What do scientists say? What did we do right? What guidelines might help us navigate? In answering the questions, Philip also pays a profound tribute to his late wife, Susan, and to the beautiful relationship they had.

—**DONNA BEARDEN,** Author of *Finding More Me: Journaling to Go Soul Deep*

"*The Essential Rules of Love* is an exceptional, well-written, and thoroughly researched guide for successful love in relationships. The use of song lyrics about love scattered through the book is moving, and I didn't realize the staggering number of love songs is well over 100 million. For anyone in a relationship, new or old, this is a guide on the scientific and biological aspects of this thing called love. After my beloved husband of thirty years died, I met a man on the dance floor in Sarasota. Never in a million years would I have dreamed I'd find another great love, let alone get married again. My new love (and now husband) Jeff said the 'F' word first: Forever. I asked him, 'How could you know?' With his right hand clenched, he tapped it on his heart saying, 'It's right here; that's how I know.' Love does complete life, and love does not die with death. . . . I believe this with my whole being. The 'ten don'ts and dos' are practical and easy to remember. This is the most complete book of love I've ever read. All stages from passion, lust, love, and longevity are covered in detail. Thank you for this wonderful read."

> —**MARIE SCOTT,** Wellness Coach, and Best-Selling Author of *Wellness Wisdom: The Holistic Guide to Revitalizing your Mind, Body and Soul,* and *How I Found Meaning (and Humor) in Widowhood, Firehouses, and Organic Vegetables: 7 Steps to Healing After Loss*

The Essential Rules of Love:
A Practical Guide to Creating a Harmonious,
Healthy, and Happy Relationship

by Philip Russotti

ISBN 978-1-64663-606-8

Published by

 köehlerbooks™

3705 Shore Drive
Virginia Beach, VA 23455
800-435-4811
www.koehlerbooks.com

The Essential Rules of

LOVE

A PRACTICAL GUIDE TO CREATING A HARMONIOUS, HEALTHY, AND HAPPY RELATIONSHIP

PHILIP RUSSOTTI

VIRGINIA BEACH
CAPE CHARLES

To Susan's memory. Without what we had
this book would not have been possible.

And to Danny and Lindsay, your mother was amazing.

Table of Contents

Foreword

This is a book born of tears and laughter.

There is certainly no shortage of authors who have tackled this subject, but few have overturned as many rocks along the way and unearthed such a wealth of insights in the process. Those of us who have managed to spend time with Mr. Russotti will attest to his resolve.

He takes us on a journey that asks for the courage to face some disquieting, albeit rewarding, truths that attend this condition we call love. He strips away many of the conventions of what we mean or think we mean when we speak of love. *The Essential Rules for Love* is an impressive foray into what at times can be an elusive and fickle quest. He can do the occasional deep dive when called for but keeps it accessible with the light touch that doesn't falter.

Mr. Russotti knows the terrain, having found for himself a life that exemplifies what he has set out to offer others. This book bears the weight of personal experience tempered by discovery and loss. It is a compelling read.

For all the light shed in this book, the author understands that understanding is not enough. Perhaps its greatest contribution lies in its practicality, working from the premise that love is ultimately an action. This book is a distillation of what couples can do and what they need not to do, and it reveals how seemingly small adjustments can have a profound effect on a relationship.

On a personal note and as a psychotherapist with a fair amount of mileage, I have sat with a good complement of couples in crisis. An honest appraisal would be to say that at times all one can do is to take out the duct tape and hope for the best . . . but much evidence exists of a genuine and at times desperate longing to improve or salvage what they have or have had.

There is an old joke that asks how many therapists it takes to change a light bulb. The answer is "only one . . . but the light bulb has to really want to change." It's very possible that in the process of changing this new light, from wherever it comes, it can illuminate for you that which is present but yet unseen.

Shakespeare said it well:

"Go to your bosom, knock there and ask your heart what it doth know."

So, readers, take heart; you are in good hands.

—*William Parker, LCSW*

Introduction

December 20, 2009, 4:00 PM, Hotel Plaza Athene, Sixty-Fourth and Madison Avenue, NYC, private room, second floor, I am sixty-one years old and standing in front of my children, their spouses, my family, and closest friends, dressed in a tuxedo, about to proclaim wedding vows to a woman to become my third wife!

What the hell was I doing? I was formalizing a relationship begun two years earlier with a woman whom I had not only fallen deeply in love with but with whom I had also developed a relationship of mutual trust, respect, admiration, caring, honesty, romance, and sexuality. I was hopeful it would continue for the rest of our lives.

That hope was realized, and the relationship lasted until Susan's untimely death from complications from ovarian cancer eight years later.

Together with extensive scientific research, I share here the lessons learned from that relationship, insights that provide hope and promise to anyone, whether in their first or fifth relationship, that a positive and mutually rewarding, loving relationship is attainable at any stage in life. The advice and analysis I offer can help anyone who has found someone new after a breakup or divorce, because it is a primer for how to do things differently the next time around. It is also helpful for anyone who feels they need to reignite the fire that has faded from a long-term relationship or for any couple that has fallen into patterns or behavior not conducive to a mutually loving relationship. Finally, this book offers hope to those who have not yet experienced the kind of relationship we will discuss.

The methodology I present is unique in the self-help-book arena because I break down love and relationships into their component parts, both functionally and pragmatically. We will begin by examining what love really is, because without understanding what it is, you won't know how to keep it. We will explore the process of love, how it develops and unfolds, and how it can transform into a lifelong relationship.

We will investigate love through the lens of an array of professionals, including psychologists, psychiatrists, philosophers, anthropologists, chemists, neuroscientists, evolutionary biologists, feminists, literary authors, and poets. We will focus on the basic components of love these disciplines encompass that influence the development, creation, and maintenance of a strong, positive relationship. You will learn from science that love develops through a combination of evolutionary forces, psychological factors, and chemical changes in the brain. You will see that these elements combine in each of us differently but can produce in all of us that wonderful feeling of wanting no one else but our beloved. We will explore the potential emotional and psychological benefits of having a loving, positive relationship that make all the work it takes worthwhile.

We will see, interspersed through the book, how love is expressed in music and poetry, which is remarkably consistent with and reflects what the researchers have found. As we will see, we inherently know many of the facets of love. And we will look at the physical aspects of love and relationships and navigate the pitfalls surrounding sex.

Finally, we will explore death and love, a topic that relationship self-help books don't cover but which I believe deserves thoughtful attention because it is something we all face. We might as well not bury our heads in the sand, and we should prepare for it.

I interweave the story of my relationship with Susan into the principles the experts espouse, explaining how we followed

professional advice unwittingly to achieve the fabulous relationship
we had. Scrutinizing our experience along with the voluminous
research I did allowed me to conclude that the principles underlying
a positive, loving relationship can effectively be reduced to
Four *Don'ts*—that I believe are at the root of most problems in
relationships—and **Six** *Dos*—that nourish and allow relationships
to grow deeper and become more fulfilling.

If you follow these rules, you will discover how to do the right
things, regardless of the stage of relationship you are in, including
how to sense the beginning of a problem and head it off before it
becomes a serious impediment to a healthy relationship. If you've made
a connection with someone with whom you envision building a life,
adhering to my *Don'ts* and *Dos* will go a long way toward helping you
arrive at a long-lasting, loving relationship.

The rules offered in this book are meant as a blueprint for fostering
and growing the relationship you desire. The earlier you follow them,
the better off you will be because they will become habits that will
define your relationship. Your life together will be built on a foundation
of respect and concern for one another. Like anything worthwhile, it
takes hard work, planning, and careful thought, and based on what
you learn here, I think you will agree it'll be worth the effort.

The title of the book, *The Essential Rules for Love*, refers to "rules"
of love. The *Dos* and *Don'ts* are written as rules. I reflected on how
the format evolved and realized that it occurred unconsciously. My
entire forty-eight-year career as a trial lawyer has dealt with rules in
every aspect of the work: rules of evidence, rules of civil procedure,
rules of voir dire, and rules of trial practice. In my effort to understand
and then explain how to have a great relationship, it was second
nature for me to take the research and my experience and codify
the advice into "rules." The "rules" of love, in this case, condense my
research and experience into easy-to-understand principles. Follow
the rules, and you will be successful in your quest. If you can't follow
the rules, you must ask yourself why not. This answer will lead you

to appreciate what you need to do in your relationship to reach the point of being able to follow the rules—because if you can't follow them, having a healthy, positive relationship will be near impossible.

If you read this book and try to follow these rules for any length of time and can't, and you *don't* find them helpful in strengthening your relationship, you may need to consider couple's counseling or individual therapy to get to the bottom of what is interfering with your efforts, or rethink whether you are with the right person. Being in a loving relationship requires having the desire and motivation to do whatever it takes to ensure its success, to do the things that nurture and advance it.

Love is manifested through action and fostered through respect. It calls for doing a variety of things for the other person, as described throughout the book, and *not* doing or saying things that disrespect them. If you can accept and abide by that premise, you have the necessary tools to create a meaningful and fulfilling relationship or rescue a flailing one and prevent a breakup, separation, or divorce.

Let's start by seeing what love is all about.

CHAPTER 1

What Is "Love"?

What is love?
Baby don't hurt me
Don't hurt me
No more

. . .

I want no other, no other lover
This is our life, our time
If we are together, I need you forever
Is it love?

("What Is Love?" Lyrics by Dee Dee Halligan and Junior Torello, 1993)

Five weeks into our relationship, on a warm August night, Susan and I were enjoying a romantic dinner on the deck of an outdoor restaurant that overlooked Three Mile Harbor Marina in East Hampton, New York, where the summer sun shimmered across the inlet's dark-blue water. Susan wore a simple white sleeveless dress that matched the sea of white tablecloths around us. She sat facing me and the water, bathed in the soft golden glow of the setting sun as it washed over her face and highlighted her beautiful blond hair that cascaded onto her shoulders. She radiated beauty and serenity. I hadn't planned to tell her how I felt about her, but as dinner unfolded and the wine flowed, the idyllic, romantic setting worked its magic on me. I leaned across the table, looked into her eyes, and softly murmured, "You know, I love you."

Susan simply smiled and nodded approvingly, saying, "I know," and that was fine with me. I was relieved that I'd laid my heart on the table and she hadn't reacted negatively, but I was also fairly certain she felt the same way and would eventually say so. To say those words and embark on a voyage without knowing where it will lead is one of the scariest parts of falling in love. Hopefully, it will be the beginning of a positive, healthy, and long-lasting love.

But many of us wonder, what exactly is "love"? We all have different ideas about what love is, but in this book I elucidate certain themes that are consistently discussed by authors and experts as I explore interesting and unique perspectives across a wide variety of fields.

Does love just happen? We all know the expression "love at first sight," which refers to the immediate or instant attraction of two people to each other that may or may not develop into the kind of relationship on which we are focused here: a permanent, committed relationship between two people for their mutual benefit and well-being. There is a scene in the film *The Godfather* that offers a dramatic example of this love-at-first-sight phenomenon. Al Pacino's character, Michael Corleone, flees to Sicily after killing a member of a rival crime family and a police captain. While there in hiding, he eyes a beautiful local woman and is struck by the "thunderbolt," as his bodyguards describe it. He and the girl instantly fall in love and marry soon after. Whether you've never seen it or simply want to refresh your memory, I recommend searching YouTube for "Thunderbolt scene in *The Godfather*" if you'd like to see a perfect fictional representation of the phenomenon known as "love at first sight."

As discussed more thoroughly in a later chapter about the science of love, experts acknowledge that love at first sight is real. Renowned biological anthropologist Helen Fisher studied the biological basis for this phenomenon and discovered, along with other researchers, that the feeling of being overtaken by love was accompanied by the immediate release of dopamine flooding a particular area of the brain.[1] This part of the brain is the reward system that generates feelings of wanting, seeking, and craving, as well as energy, focus, and motivation. Those who study or write about this topic, however, all seem to agree that this feeling does not, unfortunately, last long. That could be due to what Chris Rock humorously spells out in a standup routine about the dating representative. He says that in the early stages of a relationship, women in particular are not dating the actual person; they are dating their *representative*, the press kit of the other, not the reality: "Relationships—easy to get into, hard to maintain. Why are they so hard to maintain? Because it's hard to keep up the lie. 'Cause you can't get nobody being you. You got to lie to get somebody. You can't get nobody looking like you look, acting like you act, sounding like you sound. When you meet somebody for the first time, you're not meeting them. You're meeting their representative" (*Bigger and Blacker* HBO, 1999).

Once past the representative, you may not be so enamored by the real person.

The intense feelings triggered by love at first sight generally last six months but can last up to a year and a half or sometimes longer. One way or the other, they subside, forcing the pair to focus on "the business" of determining whether their relationship can evolve into what we generally think of as "true love." Can they continue along the path toward a lasting relationship grounded in a commitment to each other? Can they lay a lasting foundation for consistent mutual caring about the other's best interests, along with a healthy physical relationship that serves as the "emotional glue" that binds them together?

Most solid, long-term relationships don't start out with love at first sight. It's much more common for a lasting relationship to eventually evolve into love from an initial attraction or courtship

---

1   Helen Fisher, *Anatomy of Love: A Natural History of Mating, Marriage, and Why We Stray* (New York: W.W. Norton & Company, Inc., 2016), 38.

phase. In fact, between both of my marriages (before I met Susan), I was struck by the "thunderbolt" on two separate occasions, but in spite of feeling so strongly, both relationships ended disastrously, with me being the one who got hurt. Too often people discover that when the initial euphoria of love at first sight subsides, the person with whom they fell madly in love is not everything they thought they were. To be honest, Susan and I experienced "love at tenth sight." We grew into it slowly and comfortably, and though we both said the *L* word after less than two months, we had already spent a great deal of time together. It was not love at first sight.

The type of relationship we are discussing doesn't happen overnight but rather is the result of a concerted effort by two people, beginning with romantic love and ending in a lifelong commitment to each other. To accomplish this, most writers agree that "true love" is action. *It is active, not passive.* Erich Fromm, noted twentieth-century psychologist and social philosopher, as well as one of the most prolific writers on this subject, explains in *The Art of Loving* that love is an act of will: "To love somebody is not just a strong feeling—it is a decision, it is a judgment, it is a promise. If love were only a feeling, there would be no basis for the promise to love each other forever. A feeling comes and it may go."[2]

As an activity, love is primarily *giving*, not receiving. Fromm says "giving" means giving to another's joy, interest, understanding, knowledge, humor, sadness, and so on. By doing so, we enrich the other and enhance their "sense of aliveness," as Fromm calls it, because we do not give to receive but rather to experience the "exquisite joy" that is giving itself.

Fromm references American psychiatrist and psychoanalyst Harry Stack Sullivan, who maintained that "love begins when a person feels another person's needs to be as important as his own." In their book *A General Theory of Love*, eminent psychiatrists Thomas Lewis, Fari Amini, and Richard Lannon call this concept

---

2   Erich Fromm, *The Art of Loving* (New York: Harper & Row, Inc., 1956), 52.

"simultaneous mutual regulation, wherein each person meets the needs of the other."[3] They explain that this type of relationship is not fifty-fifty; it's one hundred-one hundred because each person takes perpetual care of the other, and as a result, both thrive.

Echoing this theme that love is action, psychiatrist and author M. Scott Peck, in his spiritual classic *The Road Less Traveled*, defines love as "the will to extend one's self for the purpose of nurturing one's own or another's spiritual growth." His expression "Love is as love does" is based on the idea that love is an act of will—both as intention and action.[4] He explains that will implies choice, because we don't *have* to love; we *choose* to love. Clearly, the consensus among experts is that love is not something that simply happens; it is intentional conduct directed at another that, if reciprocated, helps to make both people more complete and more capable of realizing their fullest potential.

These theories find support in the neuroscientific definition of love expressed by researchers Francesco Bianchi-Demicheli, Scott Grafton, and Stephanie Ortigue in their article "The Power of Love on the Human Brain."[5] They describe love as a complex state involving erotic, cognitive, chemical, and goal-directed behavioral components that cause the active striving for the happiness of a loved one. As I said, the scientific examination of love will be explored more deeply in chapter 5, but it is worth introducing here because it is consistent with and supports the views of the psychology experts.

Love also helps the intended beneficiary discover who they really are. Leo Buscaglia, renowned author, motivational speaker, PhD, and professor at the University of Southern California, known as "Dr. Love," believed that the essence of loving another is to assure them

---

3   Lewis Thomas, Fari Amini, and Richard Lannon, *A General Theory of Love* (New York: Random House, 2000), 208.

4   Scott M. Peck, *The Road Less Traveled: A New Psychology of Love, Traditional Values and Spiritual Growth* (New York: Touchstone, 1978), 81–83.

5   Francesco Bianchi-Demicheli, Scott Grafton, and Stephanie Ortigue, "The Power of Love on the Human Brain" *Soc Neurosci*.1(2):90-103. doi: 10.1080/17470910600976547. PMID: 18633778 (2006).

we are dedicated to their growth or realizing their limitless potential. He wrote that a couple should "use their united energies" to help each other through "the endless process of discovering who they really are, then revel forever in this continually changing knowledge and discovery." He professed that this was the only way "that human love can flourish."[6]

He provides further details: "Love, then, recognizes needs, physical and emotional. It sees as well as looks, listens as well as hears. Love touches, fondles, and revels in sensual gratification. Love is free and cannot be realized unless it is left free. Love finds its own path, sets its own pace and travels in its own way. Love recognizes and appreciates its uniqueness. Love needs no recognition, for if its effect is recognizable, it is not true love at all."[7]

Through this process, love becomes an agent of change in both persons, because one lover bestows on the other an importance commensurate with his own. Lovers express this with acts of self-sacrifice, generosity, and thoughtfulness. In *Dreams of Love and Fateful Encounters*, Ethel Spector Person, who was a professor of psychiatry at Columbia University, believed that when love is directed outward toward an "other," it provides a sense of direction, and therefore a purpose that isolated individuality lacks. This sense of direction and meaning alters our sense of self and enables us to feel capable of becoming something greater.[8] In other words, Person refers to the same capacity for change that Buscaglia expressed.

We cannot, however, be changed from the outside. We must grow from within. Interestingly, and perhaps ironically, a commitment to true love includes a commitment to allow us to change. Acclaimed American author, professor, and feminist bell hooks says that we must permit ourselves to be "acted upon by the beloved in a way

---

6   Leo Buscaglia, *Love, What Life Is All About* (New York: Random House Publishing Group, 1972), 117.

7   Ibid., 135–136.

8   Ethel Person, *Dreams of Love and Fateful Encounters: The Power of Romantic Passion* (Ontario, Canada: W.W. Norton, 1988), 122.

that enables us to be more self-actualized."[9] She goes on to say that the most common vision of true love she hears in her work is how it is "unconditional," meaning that it calls for accepting the other person as they are. But she further observes that for love to flourish, it requires an "ongoing commitment to constructive struggle and change" from within. Such a commitment demands that we make more of ourselves and become a better person toward the other in ways that advance and strengthen the relationship.

I believe that this aspect of love links our own minds and bodies with those of our partner, so that each absolutely "gets" the other in every way and encourages their self-growth and development, which then allows the other to realize their full potential. Susan and I both experienced this in many ways throughout our life together. As our bond grew, we changed and grew in our generosity toward each other, as well as toward everyone around us, especially our children. We did this not only in the giving of our time and ourselves but in "doing" for each other without being asked. Sharing generosity of spirit through our actions and deeds continually brought us closer, which our children saw and appreciated. This behavior helped my children become closer to Susan and her children closer to me, because they trusted the stability of our relationship and the example it set for them. Susan used activities, in particular cooking, pottery, and sewing, to express her love, and these activities generated love in return. Her passion for cooking, which predated our relationship, became a love of cooking for the family, which was extremely beneficial for our gatherings and the development of close familial bonds. It also enhanced our love for each other because we engaged in it as a couple, and our children witnessed this as well.

During our marriage, Susan renewed her interest in pottery, which allowed her to create beautiful vases, dishes, platters, and coasters. She sold her work at fairs, but more importantly, she shared them as gifts for family. She grew not only in her capacity as a potter and artist but

---

9   bell hooks, *All About Love* (New York: HarperCollins, 2000), 185.

in generating and receiving love, because she shared the results with all of our children. Below is a beautiful vase that she made for our home. The hearts to me represent us and our love for each other.

When my first grandson was born in 2014, Susan used the event as an opportunity to rekindle her enjoyment of sewing. She dusted off her sewing machine and began to make stuffed animals, such as dinosaurs, teddy bears, and dogs. She gave them to all the kids and to my grandson, Leonardo, now six, who still has his dinosaur in his bedroom. My children appreciated these acts of kindness because the animals were difficult to make, and they knew she had gone out of her way to make them colorful and cute.

I reciprocated this generosity of spirit and action by calling on my strengths to help her children. I started her son on his path to a career as a lawyer by suggesting that he work at my law firm as a clerk and messenger (as all my sons had done before him). That exposed him to the environment and allowed him to learn what being a lawyer was like. He soaked it up and one day told his mother he was going to law school, which, fortuitously, was her dream for him. She lived long enough to see him graduate from law school and become a successful federal court litigator. She was immensely proud.

I also gave both her children substantial monetary wedding gifts that they saved and applied to their first-home purchases. Later, when her daughter and son-in-law found a home they loved, I lent them money to enable them to successfully negotiate its purchase. I can't tell you how much those acts helped to cement my relationship with Susan. Love was the catalyst for these actions on both our parts and fostered the growth of even greater love toward each other. That we succeeded in this effort is proved by the fact that, even now, four years after Susan's death, her children and I end every conversation with "love you."

When we feel safe in our relationship with another and in being who we are, we grow inside of that relationship. Accepting the other for who they are and entering into a relationship that encourages self-change allows both individuals the freedom to achieve self-fulfillment and become the best person they can be. That is what love can be and what it can achieve for anyone willing to grow as a human being.

Here is an example of these principles involving people familiar to most, if not all, of us. The love affair and marriage of Johnny Cash and June Carter epitomized the unconditional love we have been exploring. Their expressions of love toward each other aptly demonstrated the principles the experts espouse: an ongoing commitment to change and be acted upon, a willingness to extend oneself to nurture the spiritual growth of the other and remain resolutely dedicated to their growth and accept them for who they are.

Johnny and June met behind stage at the Grand Old Opry in 1956 and were immediately attracted to each other, although at the time married to others. They began touring together in the early '60s, and presumably their relationship developed while on tour. June told *Rolling Stone* in 2000, "I never talked much about how I fell in love with John. It was not a convenient time for me to fall in love with him and it wasn't a convenient time for him to fall in love with me. . . . I was frightened of his way of life. I thought, *I can't fall in love with this man, but it's just like a ring of fire.*"

That inspired her to cowrite the hit song "Ring of Fire," which Cash recorded in 1963. After they each divorced their respective spouses in 1966 and 1967, they "officially" became a couple. In February 1968,

Johnny proposed to June onstage at the London Ice House in front of 7,000 witnesses. They married a few weeks later. Whenever asked to describe his love for June, Johnny would say "unconditional." When once asked to explain what "paradise" was, he replied, "Having coffee in the morning with June!" He credited her for helping him overcome his addictions to alcohol, amphetamines, and barbiturates and always being there for him during his numerous stays in and out of rehab and for staying by his side when he was clean to encourage him. Cash told *Rolling Stone*, "She loves me in spite of everything, in spite of myself. She has saved my life more than once. . . . She's always been there with her love and it has certainly made me forget the pain for a long time, many times." She complemented those thoughts by saying she never regretted being with him and sometimes neglected her career for him: "I've always walked along right by his side, and he's always supported everything I do." They remained together for over thirty years.

June died in May 2003, and Johnny gave his final concert that July. He was visibly frail but nevertheless honored June between songs: "The spirit of June Carter overshadows me tonight with the love she had for me and the love I have for her. We connected somewhere between here and Heaven. She came down for a short visit, I guess, from Heaven to visit with me tonight to give me courage and inspiration, like she always has. . . . I thank God for June Carter. I love her with all my heart." Johnny passed away two months later.

That's what love is.

CHAPTER 2

The Benefits of Love

The greatest thing you'll ever learn
Is just to love and be loved in return.

("Nature Boy," Eden Ahbez, 1948)

N ow that we've explored what love is, you might be asking, "Is it worth it?" By all accounts, creating a long-lasting, loving relationship takes a lot of hard work, determination, and commitment, so it's logical to wonder what could possibly make all that effort worthwhile. The *benefits*, discussed in this chapter, are what make it worthwhile.

On an existential level, Erich Fromm postulates that love is the only sane response to the problem of human existence. He explains that because humans possess reason, we have the self-awareness to know that we are a separate entity in the world. We are aware of our short life span, that we had no say in being born and may die either before those we love or after them, and that we have little control over this condition. Fromm contends that this helplessness against the forces of nature makes existence an "unbearable prison." To cope with this realization, humans reach out to the world around them. For Fromm, then, "the deepest need of man . . . is the need to overcome his separateness, to leave the prison of his aloneness."[10]

---

10   Erich Fromm, *The Art of Loving* (New York: Harper & Row, Inc., 1956), 9.

The question becomes, *how* do we do this?

The history of religion and philosophy includes our endless attempts to cope with this predicament. For Fromm, the answer lies in "the achievement of interpersonal union with another person, in *love*." He believes that the desire for this union with another is the "force which keeps the human race together, the clan, the family, society." In fact, this desire is so fundamental he asserts that "without love, humanity could not exist for a day." Fromm maintains that love is the only answer to the emptiness of life. It is an active power that unites each of us with others for the purpose of overcoming innate isolation and separateness. In love, "the paradox occurs that two beings become one and yet remain two."[11]

So the first benefit of love is that it helps us overcome Fromm's "unbearable prison" of aloneness. I can think of no greater benefit.

This theme is echoed in the writings of Ethel Person, who believed that love confers freedom from the "confines of the self."[12] Love replaces self-preoccupation with a consuming interest in the *other*. This deep interest includes aspects of the other's character that might otherwise be insignificant—idiosyncrasies and habits, for example—but which take on a heightened importance and meaning within the bubble of love. What was once insignificant becomes important because our partner notices and appreciates it. For instance, it is not that she wears perfume but the specific perfume she uses that takes on increased importance. She becomes aware of his mannerisms because she regards them with affection. When this process occurs, we are validated because all of our attributes are noted and are affirmed by our beloved. In becoming the object of love, "our insecurities are healed, our importance guaranteed only when we become the object of love."[13] Simply put, we feel "seen."

Mutual love also creates a new entity. It is not just the other who is celebrated or the "I" that is enhanced; there is a new being

---

11   Ibid., 19.
12   Ethel Person, *Dreams of Love and Fateful Encounters: The Power of Romantic Passion* (Ontario, Canada: W.W. Norton, 1988), 38.
13   Ibid., 59.

jointly experienced as "we" and perceived by others as a "couple." The "couple" is the first child of the union. It has a birthday and its own anniversaries—the day the couple met, the day they first went out, the day they first slept together, the day they married, and so on. The "we" accumulates its own history. This new entity even has its own mutual secrets that are rooted in intimacy, trust, and commitment, and which serve to strengthen the bonds between the two individuals.

So a second benefit of love is the creation of a new space for lovers to occupy that serves as a buffer against the outside world, providing them comfort and safety where they are free to express their most private thoughts without fear of recrimination. The development of such a relationship makes life not only more enjoyable and worthwhile but helps us feel protected and secure from outside influences. It forms a shelter from the outside world, a benefit surely worth the effort.

For a more spiritual viewpoint on how love benefits us as humans, consider Thomas Merton, an American Trappist monk and theologian who wrote about the transformative power of love in his essay "Love and Need." Merton believed that love completes life. He proposed that communion with another and the concept of self-transcendence are why we come into the world. He explains that we "do not become fully human until we give ourselves to each other in love," and "love is our true destiny. We do not find the meaning of life ourselves alone—we find it with another."[14] While these may be lofty ideas, they are included as a third benefit of a committed relationship because they add a new and powerful dimension to our discussion.

Maryanne Fisher, professor of psychology at St. Mary's University in Halifax, Canada, and prolific author on the evolutionary basis of interpersonal relationships, expands on this theme from a more down-to-earth perspective. She observes that even without the desire to have children, there exists a universal human desire, rooted in evolution,

---

14   Thomas Merton, *Love and Living*, Edited by Naomi Burton Stone and Brother Patrick Hart (New York: Farrar, Straus and Giroux, 1979), 27.

to have the physical and emotional companionship of another. Fisher explains that evolutionary forces underlie the instinct to settle down to nurture offspring, forces that still manifest themselves today.[15] Ethel Person, too, contends that love gives life a sense of direction and purpose, which is lacking in isolated individuality. Person says this sense of direction and meaning further alters our sense of self, enabling us to become something more than we thought we could be. Achieving mutual love is often "accompanied by spurts of energy, growth, and change and by a sense of richness and abundance."[16]

On a more practical level, Fisher points out that couples that live together in love have in one another at once a lover, a principal companion, a sounding board, a coparent, and a housemate.[17] To be all of these things requires that each member of the couple invest an enormous amount of energy in the other and take on the tremendous responsibility of sustaining that energy. But doing so offers an unparalleled opportunity for growth and change, with the possibility of living a rich, full, and rewarding life together. In *A General Theory of Love*, Thomas Lewis and his coauthors expand on this concept by explaining that each partner takes perpetual care of the other, and because of this reciprocity, both thrive: "For those who attain it, the benefits of deep attachment are powerful—regulated people feel whole, centered, alive . . . they are resilient to the stresses of daily life, or even to those of extraordinary circumstances."[18]

This ability to thrive and to be resilient is a fourth benefit of a strong long-term relationship.

The truth is we don't need a psychiatrist, therapist, theologian, or

---

15   Maryanne L. Fisher, Justin R. Garcia, and Rosemarie Sokol Chang, Editors, *Evolution's Empress, Darwinian Perspectives on the Nature of Women* (New York: Oxford Univ. Press, 2013).

16   Ethel Spector Person, *Dreams of Love and Fateful Encounters: The Power of Romantic Passion* (Ontario, Canada: W.W. Norton, 1988), 99.

17   Maryanne Fisher and Victoria Costello, *The Complete Idiot's Guide to the Chemistry of Love* (New York: Penguin Group, 2010), 57.

18   Thomas Lewis, Fari Amini, and Richard Lannon, *A General Theory of Love* (New York: Random House, 2000), 208.

philosopher to explain the benefits of love to us. Love has been the subject of songs, poems, and literature since the dawn of language and writing, expressed by lyricists, poets, writers, and yes, even lawyers turned authors. For me, the utter joy of being in love is best expressed in the song "My One and Only Love," played by John Coltrane and sung by Johnny Hartman. The lyrics convey the exquisite nature of being truly in love:

> *The very thought of you makes my heart sing*
> *Like the April breeze on the wings of spring*
> *And you appear in all your splendor*
> *My one and only love*
>
> *The shadows fall and spread their mystic charms*
> *In the hush of night while you're in my arms*
> *I feel your lips, so warm and tender*
> *My one and only love*
>
> *The touch of your hand is like heaven*
> *A heaven that I've never known*
> *The blush on your cheek whenever I speak*
> *Tells me that you are my own*
>
> *You fill my eager heart with such desire*
> *Every kiss you give sets my soul on fire*
> *I give my heart in sweet surrender*
> *My one and only love*
> *My one and only love*

(Lyrics by Guy Wood and Robert Mellin, 1952)

I confess that this was our wedding song, and some of the lyrics were my vows to her. The line "you fill my heart with such desire, every kiss you give sets my soul on fire" is to me one of the most profound and succinct metaphors for love I have ever come across. In a later chapter, we will discuss the concept of "savoring," which is talking about your love for each other, a technique recommended to reinforce the love you share. This song is a wonderful example of "savoring," written long before that was recognized as a psychological concept. Sharing words like these, even if you didn't write them but rather adopted them, cannot help but be beneficial to any relationship. I would often play this song on Sunday mornings, and Susan would simply smile. Nothing else needed to be said. It was a reminder of our wedding ceremony and how I felt about her. Playing the song made us feel good about "savoring" our relationship.

Poetry famously and frequently extols the benefits of love. Poets often show great insight into love, perhaps because they tend to be more sensitive or closely attuned to their emotions. But we all know on some level what love should be and what we want it to be, and we simply need a little guidance now and then to achieve it. Our personal issues can get in the way of recognizing love, but this book will help set those aside so you can concentrate on your relationship as a couple and foster love between the two of you. Poet Kerry DeVore, in "God's Gift to Me," beautifully expresses some of the more visceral benefits of love:

You are my sunshine.
You are my shining star.
Everything I'm not,
You are.

You make me laugh.
You make my heart smile.
Everything you do
Makes life worthwhile.

You give lovingly.
You always have cheer.
Everything you are
I hold dear.

You are so sweet.
You are so very kind.
Everything I cherish,
In you I find.

You are a blessing.
You are an angel I see.
Everything about you
Is God's gift to me.

What greater benefit can there be than being a "blessing" to your love?

Psychologists, psychiatrists, theologians, evolutionary biologists, authors, songwriters, singers, and poets all recognize the enormous benefits of real love. That is a strong endorsement for diving deeper into what it takes to achieve a loving, long-term relationship. In the next chapter, we'll explore the process that takes you from your first meeting to falling in love to exploring ways to help build the lifelong relationship that so many of us are eager to experience.

CHAPTER 3

The Process of Love

I loved you first: but afterward your love
Outsoaring mine, sang such a loftier song . . .
Which owes the other most? My love was long,
And yours one moment seemed to wax more strong

. . .

For verily love knows not 'mine' or 'thine'
With separate 'I' and 'thou' free love has done,
For one is both and both are one in love;
Rich love knows nought of 'thine that is not mine'

. . .

Both of us, of the love which makes us one.

("I Loved You First: But Afterwards Your Love" by Christina Rossetti)

We've already touched on some of the elements of the process of love and how it develops, including the phenomenon of "love at first sight." But whether love begins there or develops over time, most can agree that there are generally recognized phases of love, so it's worthwhile to examine these in greater detail.

Dr. Person explains that the first step in the process of love occurs when an individual begins to fall in love, and his or her thoughts and fantasies drift involuntarily toward the object of his or her love, followed shortly thereafter by repetitive, even obsessive, thinking about the other. This preoccupation is most often experienced as a "high," one in which the lover feels swept up in powerful emotions and a consuming interest in the other. Fits and starts of desire are often followed by feelings of doubt about the other's loyalty and their mutual interest in pursuing the same path. Vacillation between these two states continues until the lovers either pledge loyalty to each other or one of them gives up the pursuit.

This phase can be described as a "campaign" of sorts, waged with flowers, dinners, letters (or emails), cards, and a variety of other special kindnesses, as the pursuer attempts to convince the object of affection to join the quest for mutual love. Experts and laypeople alike agree that this stage usually involves idealization of the object of love to the point where they value every physical and emotional characteristic of the other. Person suggests that idealization does not mean that love is blind, only that the lover's appraisal of the other diverges from that of "objective" acquaintances because the lover imbues his object with traits beyond the obvious. While the beloved may not be the most beautiful, her face is more interesting, and it reveals her soul; others may be smarter, but he is more sensitive; others might be more successful, but she is more charitable; and so on. Person explains that the reason loving feels so good is because it is so creative in this way.[19]

In *Can Love Last?*, psychoanalytic theorist Stephen Mitchell discusses Sigmund Freud's view of idealization, called "overvaluation," a mindset where we attribute an illusory value to how we see another person.[20] For Mitchell, this only means that the object of your desire is no ordinary person but rather someone special and unique. It becomes the stuff of infatuation, a kind of magical spell that transforms the mundane into something transcendent. Mitchell deems idealization, itself central to romantic love, the source of both

---

19   Ethel Spector Person, *Dreams of Love and Fateful Encounters: The Power of Romantic Passion* (Ontario, Canada: W.W. Norton, 1988), 42–45.

20   Stephen Mitchell, *Can Love Last, The Fate of Romance Over Time* (New York: W.W. Norton & Company, 2002), 95.

its magic and its fragility, because ideals can so easily be tarnished. In other words, idealization is childlike behavior laced with fantasy, which can fade when familiarity and a more realistic view of the other, "warts and all," settle in. The idealization that fuels romantic love cannot be maintained indefinitely and begins to fade once we see the other person for who they are.[21] Traditional psychoanalytic theory takes a dim view of this romantic stage of love because it is regressive and childlike. In Mitchell's view, romantic love is best regarded as a prelude to a more stable love. Once reality intervenes, the lover can begin to see the other person objectively. We can then hope that this infatuation stage will be transformed into one that instead displays a more sober "liking" of the other.[22]

In her book *Anatomy of Love*, Dr. Helen Fisher, biological anthropologist and expert in the science of human attraction, examines this period of intrusive thoughts. She cites a study in which participants spent from 85 to almost 100 percent of their time thinking about the object of their love and as a result lost the ability to concentrate on daily tasks like work and school. Fisher also describes "crystallization," a process distinct from idealization, in which the infatuated person recognizes the weaknesses in the other but simply ignores them or convinces themselves that the weaknesses are unique or charming![23]

Fisher identifies negative feelings that occur at this stage, e.g., shyness, anticipation, fear of rejection, longing for reciprocity, and jealousy, all promoted by the intense motivation to win this special person. Fisher aptly describes this part of the process: "Romantic love, it seems, is a panoply of intense emotions, roller-coastering from high to low, hinged to the pendulum of a single being whose whims command you to the detriment of everything around you—

---

21 Ibid.

22 Ibid., 94.

23 Helen Fisher, *Anatomy of Love: A Natural History of Mating, Marriage, and Why We Stray* (New York: W.W. Norton & Company, Inc., 2016), 21.

including work, family and friends."[24]

Consider for example a person sitting at work, unable to concentrate because they are obsessed with hearing from their lover. *Why hasn't she called or texted me in the last two hours? What's she doing? Has she started to lose interest? Am I overreacting?* Then when the text finally lands, the heart races with anticipation to make sure every word is positive, that nothing is wrong, and that there is no change in direction of the relationship. The text is read ad nauseam to make sure it conveys interest and sincerity. Maybe he begins to interpret the words, project his insecurities into their meaning. *What is she really trying to say? How do I respond without betraying my insecurity?* For many of us, this is familiar territory during the early stage of romantic relationships, either from our own experiences or what we hear from friends or family.

If this first phase of falling in love is successful and reciprocated, we move to the next stage, the creation of a new entity: the "couple." As introduced in chapter 2, this entity has a birthday (the day you met), anniversaries (first date or the day you first slept together, etc.), and so on. As Person describes it, this is when the couple delights in recounting stories of shared events, along with other things they did together for the first time. Places they visit are "theirs" to the extent that if they separate, these places may become sacred, not to be visited with a future lover. The couple may have their own language, with pet names and other words or phrases that become a private way of communicating, symbolizing the uniqueness of their relationship. Together the couple creates their own secrets, rooted in intimacy, trust, and commitment.[25]

One year into our relationship, Susan and I had created a catalogue of shared and valued experiences that we often talked about. Over a dinner out, we'd recount prior experiences, like what I thought

---

24   Ibid., 22.
25   Ethel Spector Person, *Dreams of Love and Fateful Encounters: The Power of Romantic Passion* (Ontario, Canada: W.W. Norton, 1988), 62.

of how she looked the first time we met, how romantic our first dinner together was, and how I tried to pick a particularly romantic restaurant. We talked about when we went dancing at Salsa Night at Lincoln Center's Summer Dancing on the Plaza. Even though neither of us knew what we were doing, we salsa-danced wildly, honoring the principle that we should "dance as if no one's watching." Every time we recounted the story, we laughed about how, as I later learned, a judge I frequently appeared in front of saw us, leaving me mortified that I'd replaced my serious persona of a dignified attorney with the dancing fool. Susan dubbed him "The Dancing Judge" whenever we referred to this incident. We never stopped adding to this rich private collection of stories. They remained a source both of amusement and cement for the foundation of our relationship.

As the journey of love continues, passion tends to wane because of familiarity and "habituation," which Stephen Mitchell believes "kills desire." Habituation, according to Mitchell, is a consequence of love's developmental history. He advises that habituation must be overcome for the relationship to remain fresh.[26] Avoiding that pitfall leads to what Person calls "affectionate bonding," which may or may not be combined with sexuality. Affectionate bonding is the product of ongoing happiness, where the couple learns, develops, and discovers their shared values, habits, and pleasures. The partners have arrived at a realistic appreciation of one another and are secure in each other's commitment to the relationship. They validate each other's lives, and this provides warmth not only for themselves but for family and friends around them.[27]

Susan and I achieved this with each other and our respective families. We each came to a complete understanding of the other: our values, likes, dislikes, strengths, and weaknesses. I knew Susan was very private, introspective, and soft spoken. She knew I was

---

26   Stephen A. Mitchell, *Can Love Last, The Fate of Romance Over Time* (New York: W.W. Norton & Company, 2002), 45.

27   Ethel Spector Person, *Dreams of Love and Fateful Encounters: The Power of Romantic Passion* (Ontario, Canada: W.W. Norton, 1988), 325.

more outgoing, spontaneous, transparent, and, on occasion, loud. She had "class" and always carried herself with dignity and grace. In fact, her role model was Grace Kelly, the actress who gave up a wildly successful movie career to marry the prince of Monaco and become a princess. Kelly was beautiful, refined, genteel, dignified, and always impeccably dressed, characteristics Susan strove to emulate. By contrast, I am rough around the edges, boisterous, and prone to outbursts derisive of people or things that irritate me. Neither of us tried to change the other, although you might be wondering why I would ever want to change her in the first place. I didn't, of course. But even though she probably should have tried to change me, the most she did was ask me to turn down music I habitually played too loudly. As my stepson observes, this does not mean we did not change *because* of one another. Hers was a calming influence on me, while she became more outgoing. We met in the middle, a natural and unforced consequence of our love. As *our* love process developed, we became secure in who we were as individuals and who we were as a couple. That confidence cemented our relationship into an incredibly strong and mutually supportive bond.

So, what brings two people together in the first place? Any discussion of the way love develops is bound to raise this question. Without wading into the deep psychological waters of Freudian psychoanalytic theory, we should simply acknowledge his view that the degree and quality of your early emotional attachments to your parents, most notably your mother, will likely influence your attractions later in life.[28] The infant–mother bond is considered the most significant relationship we have in terms of its impact on our ability to form strong and healthy relationships. It is commonly thought in Freudian psychology that we are attracted to potential mates who are most like the parent with whom we have unresolved issues because we have a subconscious need to work out these issues

---

28   Maryanne Fisher and Victoria Costello, *The Complete Idiot's Guide to the Chemistry of Love* (New York: Penguin Group, 2010).

as adults. This is the bread and butter of every psychoanalyst's practice.

For our purposes, we can turn to Helen Fisher, who succinctly summarizes the psychological issues that play into this question of attraction. She believes that we all develop a "love map," or an unconscious list of traits that we are looking for in our ideal partner.[29] This map begins in early childhood (between five and eight years old) in response to family, friends, and experiences in and out of the house, when we are exposed to temperaments and personalities of those with whom we come into contact and which create unconscious patterns in our minds about what turns us on and off. During puberty, when sexual feelings flood the brain, our love map solidifies, and more details are added, such as body type, temperament, humor, and personality. This mapping process depicts who we are likely to be attracted to in later years. In the timeless words of the Rolling Stones, "[We] can't always get what [we] want, but [we] can get what [we] need." Thus the process may involve compromising on some aspects of our prospective "perfect" mate. Dating helps crystallize which characteristics are the most important facets of our love map, because we all have our own "must-haves," but they are different for everyone. No one person will have all the traits we seek, so we experiment to find out which ones are most important to each of us.

While the well-known expression "opposites attract" may be true for some people, Maryanne Fisher cites studies indicating that people are, in fact, attracted to those who are similar to themselves in some way, known as homogamy—i.e., "birds of a feather flock together."[30] We tend to place greater importance on characteristics that we ourselves possess. For example, we are more likely to marry those within the same socioeconomic group or within the same ethnicity or religion. Fisher theorizes that homogamy may be a key to happiness, stability, and satisfaction in a relationship. The

---

29   Helen Fisher, *Anatomy of Love: A Natural History of Mating, Marriage, and Why We Stray* (New York: W.W. Norton & Company, Inc., 2016), 26.
30   Maryanne L. Fisher, Editor, *The Oxford Handbook of Women and Competition* (New York: Oxford Univ. Press, 2017), 283.

evolution of my relationship with Susan validates this theory. At first, I was merely physically attracted to Susan, but once I witnessed her devotion to her children, I recognized a trait I valued and shared above all others, that family must be a priority. I consciously said to myself, *Here is a woman with the same values*, which strongly influenced my decision to pursue her.

Maryanne Fisher asserts that being attracted to someone is the result of a combination of chemistry, psychology, and evolution, all of which interact to influence our attraction to a particular person, with no one factor predominating. She reports that the most current scientific thinking about love and sexuality is that the mind and body are one big feedback loop. The chemistry of attraction (which will be discussed later) doesn't happen in a vacuum. The chemicals secreted in our brains that drive the attraction and obsessive compulsion for the other person do so in response to environmental, cultural, and psychological factors within the context of who we are as a whole person.[31] Given that we are all unique products of our backgrounds and experiences, it follows that our influences and paths to love are different.

Finally, Thomas Lewis and his coauthors explain that the development of a committed relationship requires time. They believe that too many people spend their lives searching for love because they haven't been taught the "simple equations of love." In other words, "relationships live on time. They devour it in the way that bees feed on pollen or aerobic cells on oxygen: with an unbending singularity of purpose and no possibility of compromise or substitution." Growing into a relationship is a "physiologic process that, like digestion or bone growth" cannot be artificially accelerated. The authors explain that being attuned to your partner's emotional rhythms requires an investment of years.[32] To be sure, the process of

---

31   Maryanne Fisher and Victoria Costello, *The Complete Idiot's Guide to the Chemistry of Love* (New York, Penguin Group, 2010), 64.
32   Thomas Lewis, Fari Amini, and Richard Lannon, *A General Theory of Love* (New York: Random House, 2000), 205.

developing a lasting, committed, and healthy relationship requires, in addition to all the other factors we've discussed, time.

Having an understanding of the nature of love, how its benefits are worth the effort, and an appreciation for the intricacies of developing a loving relationship, it's time to examine the difficulties we must overcome to attain that relationship.

CHAPTER 4

Difficulties of Finding Love

'Cause I can't make you love me if you don't
You can't make your heart feel something it won't
Here in the dark, in these final hours
I will lay down my heart and I'll feel the power
But you won't, no you won't
'Cause I can't make you love me, if you don't

("I Can't Make You Love Me"; Lyrics by Allen Shamblin and Mike Reid 1991;
popularized by Emmylou Harris)

I n this chapter, we will focus on difficulties we encounter when searching for a lifelong relationship. The first is the realization that attaining a permanently satisfying, healthy relationship is in itself a challenging undertaking. Leo Buscaglia observed (almost fatalistically) that "we seem to refuse to face the obvious fact that most of us spend our lives trying to find love, trying to live in it and dying without ever truly discovering it." He argues that many of us play at love, imitate lovers, and treat love as a game, which explains why so many die lonely or otherwise feel anxious and unfulfilled even in seemingly close relationships, continually searching for more in life.[33] Given our society's obsession with love and the attention it gets in literature, poetry, music, art, dance, psychology, science,

---

33   Leo Buscaglia, *Love, What Life is All About* (New York:, Random House Publishing Group, 1972), 35.

psychiatry, and sociology, Buscaglia was likely correct, which speaks volumes about how difficult it is to attain. What a sad predicament! One wonders how, then, our goal can even be achieved.

On the positive side, however, everything created in the name of love is a testament to the resilience and determination of the human spirit. Perhaps Erich Fromm was correct in believing love is the only thing that gives meaning to our existence and is therefore the driving force behind our continual efforts to find what Buscaglia believes is so elusive. In *The Art of Loving*, Erich Fromm observes that "there is hardly any activity . . . which is started with such tremendous hopes and expectations, and yet, which fails so regularly, as love."[34] This may be because, as Stephen Mitchell observes, "our longing for safety and our thirst for passion pulls us in opposite directions," placing us in a precarious and dissonant position. Those feelings that cause us to idealize the other "may not be reciprocated; love may remain unrequited."[35] Rather than being synchronous, love usually begins in one individual. As Fromm explains, "Love means to commit oneself without guarantee, to give oneself completely in the hope that our love will produce love in the loved person"[36] To love is therefore to make ourselves vulnerable and risk pain because, as Thomas Lewis says, "love cannot be extracted, commanded, demanded or wheedled. It can only be given."[37] It begins in one person, who is vulnerable until the love that is given is either returned or rejected by the recipient.

You don't have to be a psychiatrist or philosopher to appreciate that love can't be forced, no matter how hard we try. As I revealed earlier, twice I fell madly in love with women who preferred to live their lives without me. Unrequited love is not uncommon. It happens to most of us at one time or another.

---

34   Erich Fromm, *The Art of Loving* (New York, Harper & Row, Inc., 1956), 4.
35   Stephen A. Mitchell, *Can Love Last, The Fate of Romance Over Time* (New York, W.W. Norton & Company, 2002), 113.
36   Erich Fromm, *The Art of Loving* (New York, Harper & Row, Inc., 1956).
37   Thomas Lewis, Fari Amini, and Richard Lannon, *A General Theory of Love* (New York: Random House, 2000), 2.

A second difficulty in truly and honestly loving is the idea, agreed upon by experts and nonexperts alike, that before you can love another, you must love yourself. As Buscaglia explains, this means having a genuine interest, caring, concern, and respect for oneself. A man loves himself when he can see himself accurately and realistically appreciate what he sees but is excited and challenged by the prospect of what he can become. The search for love should challenge us not only to be good, loving, feeling, and intelligent but to be the best, most loving, most feeling, and most intelligent person we are capable of being. Loving yourself involves the discovery of the true wonder of you, not only the present you, but the many possibilities of you. Echoing Buscaglia on this subject, bell hooks tells us that we can never love anyone else if we are unable to love ourselves, because we can't give what we don't have. She believes, as so many others do, that we can't expect to receive the love from someone else that we do not give to ourselves.[38]

Hooks agrees, believing hope springs eternally, which is consistent with the premise of this book, as well as what Susan and I experienced. "The light of love is always in us," she says, "no matter how cold the flame. It is always present, waiting for the spark to ignite, waiting for the heart to awaken and call us back to the first memory of being the life force inside a dark place waiting to be born—waiting to see the light."[39] Match.com, eHarmony, Tinder, Bumble, speed dating, modern-day matchmakers, and all the other online and offline dating services are a testament to the enduring human desire to find love, regardless of age, temperament, social status, or position in life, and they also illustrate that it's never too late.

Susan and I are poster children for hooks's encouraging outlook. We met as a result of a Craigslist ad I posted in the personals section. To stand out from all the other ads, I began with "Summer Share East Hampton, private bedroom and bath on nicely wooded property,

---

38   bell hooks, *All About Love* (New York: HarperCollins, 2000), 68.
39   Ibid., 68.

reasonable rent." Then I added, "BTW, I am divorced, like dining at fine restaurants, dancing, and gardening . . . who knows what can happen?" I received many responses but only replied to Susan's, and the rest is history.

She and I exchanged friendly emails for a few days before I invited her to join me and two friends of mine (not a couple) for dinner and dancing. Being a cautious and clever woman, Susan asked to meet me ahead of time at the bar of the restaurant where we were meeting my friends, so if I turned out to be an "axe murderer" (as she used to say when later recounting the story to others), she could make a quick getaway. Thankfully, no getaway was needed. The four of us spent a lovely evening together, and it was a great way to take the pressure off of having to make first-date conversation.

One of the greatest difficulties is knowing when to say "I love you" to your partner. This is a potential roadblock in the journey to a long-term, stable relationship. Ironically, merely uttering the words *I love you* is charged with emotional gravity, and saying it for the first time is one of the greatest risks to take in a relationship. When not reciprocated early on, it can jeopardize the relationship. Being out on the I-love-you limb, waiting for a response, is a frightening prospect for anyone.

Seinfeld captured the dilemma with its characteristic humor. The scene is in Jerry's apartment when George tells Jerry and Elaine he wants to tell his new girlfriend he loves her.

George: "I'm thinking of making a big move."

Jerry: "What?"

George: "I might . . . tell her . . . that I love her."

Jerry: "Oh, my."

George: "I came this close last night"—gesturing with two pinched fingers—"and I chickened out."

Jerry: "That's a big move, Georgie-boy. Are you confident in the 'I love you' return?"

George: "Fifty-fifty."

Jerry: "Because if you don't get that return, that's a pretty big matzo ball hanging out there."

On his next date, while he and his girlfriend are sitting in his car listening to a hockey game he turned down to be with her, George struggles to get the words out, but eventually stammers, "I love you." His girlfriend instinctively turns to him and responds, "I'm hungry; let's get something to eat." The matzo ball has landed.

As Stephen Mitchell explains, when two people say "I love you" to each other, it is not just a report on what is happening between them but rather contributes to determining what they can become for each other and "whether and how their relationship may deepen and whether certain paths of development will be foreclosed."[40] It changes the dynamic of the relationship and will either propel it further along if reciprocated or, as George Costanza learned, signal its death knell.

As humorously depicted by the cartoon below, the dilemma is real and present in most new relationships. When to say it, whether it should have been said long ago, or shouldn't be said so soon are not theoretical concerns but worries much agonized over by many.

"I told you, nothing is wrong"

---

40   Stephen A. Mitchell, *Can Love Last, The Fate of Romance Over Time* (New York: W.W. Norton & Company, 2002), 196.

Now you're probably wondering when the right time is to say these words. The answer, unfortunately, is that there is no definitive right or wrong time. The problem is that if "I love you" is uttered too soon, you risk seeming needy, desperate, or misjudging the other person's commitment, but waiting too long may erroneously signal that you are not interested in furthering the relationship or in making a commitment, which could cause the other to question the time and effort they have put into the relationship. The good news is that there are some guidelines that can help. For example, if your overtures of affection are being continually reciprocated, if you're spending most or all of your free time together, if you've discussed being exclusive and exploring whether you have a future together, these can all be indications that it could be a logical time to take that leap of faith, wear your heart on your sleeve, and just put it out there.

The night I told Susan I loved her, I had no intention of springing it on her when we sat down to dinner. At that point in our relationship, we both knew what was going on and what was bubbling beneath the surface, but nothing had been verbalized. As I described in chapter 1, as we sat at the table, I instinctively felt that the setting and the atmosphere had created the perfect opportunity to cross the Rubicon and lay it out there. For me, there was nothing logical about it. It was a spontaneous outpouring of emotion. I remember not thinking about it long. It entered my consciousness that this would be the ideal time to say it, and that little voice in my head immediately spoke to me, saying, "Let's do this," and out came the words. One of the best decisions in my life took only seconds to make!

I was surprised to learn during the writing of this book that while people *think* women are more likely to say "I love you" first, empirical evidence cited by *Psychology Today* and corroborated by additional research shows the opposite: men do it first, at a rate of about three to one, some even within the first month of dating. Women are more likely to be cautious and hold back.[41] Consistent with this research but also true to her reserved personality, Susan didn't reciprocate until a couple of weeks later, while we sat alone on the beach. But once she did, it cemented our desire to move forward together. In the end, while there's no clear advice on when to say "I love you," it's important to carefully consider the consequences beforehand, because your impulse to move forward could have the opposite effect on the relationship. If you expect too much in return, you risk being devastated; if you move too fast and take your lover by surprise, they could turn off and start to back away instead of moving closer. Those three small words can either move the relationship forward or put the brakes on it, so do not trivialize the significance of the right time to say them.

Another great difficulty we face in finding love in our relationships is different partner approaches toward money. Tax and financial advisor Walter Primoff warns, "A spendthrift spouse married to a saver typically creates relationship-destroying issues."[42] In other words, money issues are serious matters. Primoff and every other writer on the topic suggest that couples should fully discuss money and their values and habits about handling it before they enter into a committed relationship. As dramatic as this may sound, psychotherapist Susan Winslow advises that "it's simply better not to marry someone who has money problems, or financial habits, ideas, and values that are very different from your own."[43] You can devise any kind of system you want, from pooling your money into one account to which you both have equal access to each having your own bank account along with a joint one for shared expenses, to any variation on which you can both

41   M. A. Harrison and J. C. Shortall, "Women and Men in Love: Who Really Feels it and Says it First?" *The Journal of Social Psychology*, (2011): 151, 727–736; J. M. Ackerman, V. Griskevicius, and N. P. Li, *Let's Get Serious: Communicating Commitment in Romantic Relationships. Journal of Personality and Social Psychology 100* (2011): 1079–1094.
42   Walter Primoff, *Your Best Tips for Managing the Family Money, New York Times* (June 26, 2019).
43   David Pogue, "Your Best Tips for Managing the Family Money," (quoting Susan Winslow), *New York Times*, June 26, 2019.

agree. The important thing is to agree on a system ahead of time. This system will, to a large extent, be influenced by your personal values and habits with regard to money.

Having such a prearranged system in place will prevent money issues from interfering with the development and maintenance of a loving relationship. An excellent self-help book for money management is Nathan Dungan's *Money Sanity Solutions: An Interactive Guide to Help Your Family Build Healthy Money Habits.*[44] Dungan has helped thousands of families over the past twenty years to align their money decisions with their values. His book has a series of questions to work on as a couple to help determine your money temperament, i.e., are you a spender, saver, or sharer, and how do you handle your money, etc. He helps you explore your money values, including the differences between what you feel are your needs versus your wants, and how those values affect your money decisions. He provides aids to help with budgeting, to determine what kind of consumer you are, what kind of vacations you like, how to evaluate the cost of technology, how to save, what your values about spending around holidays and special occasions are, and how the way you pay for things affects what you spend.

The critical takeaway is to have these discussions openly and honestly before you move in together or tie the knot. But even if you're already together and have never had this talk, it's never too late to have these discussions to iron out any differences so that money management does not become a significant and troublesome issue. Susan and I had these conversations going into our relationship because we both had incomes and assets and wanted to preserve them for our children. When Susan moved into my co-op apartment, and throughout our ten years together, we kept our incomes separate, and I continued to pay all expenses. We only pooled our resources in connection with the beach house we purchased together a year after we met. But first

---

44   Nathan Dungan, *Money Sanity Solutions* (Minneapolis: Share Save Spend, 2010).

we had a serious discussion in which we both agreed that we owned the property fifty-fifty and that each person's share would go to their children should one of us die. We set up the deed to ensure that would happen. We equally split expenses on the house, using a joint checking account into which we both deposited funds.

After Susan became sick and couldn't earn at the same level she had been earning, she still wanted to contribute, so we agreed to reduce her contribution to what she felt comfortable with depending on her income, but she kept her equity share at 50 percent. After her death, her children each owned one-fourth of the house, and I owned the other half. They preferred that I buy them out, so I had the house appraised, took out a mortgage for 50 percent of the value, and paid them their mother's share with the proviso that they could continue to use the house anytime they wanted. They still have their own bedrooms and use the house whenever they wish.

The important thing is that we discussed everything and agreed to it beforehand, so money was never an issue. I proposed marriage in 2009, two years to the day that we met. Susan had never uttered the *M* word, but I wanted to fully solidify our relationship. We had frank discussions about our finances beforehand, which resulted in a postnuptial agreement, in which we both waived any right to the other's assets so that our respective property could pass to our respective children. Discussing money up front, before commitments are made, is the best way to avoid having it interfere with the solid, long-term relationship you want to develop.

The difficulties involved in the quest to enjoy a lifetime of love, but the enduring desire among humans to pursue it regardless, are proved by the sea of self-help books on relationships and love. This industry reinforces bell hooks's perspective—namely, that we are not born knowing how to love and that many people don't have a clue about how to do it.[45] This sentiment is also echoed by Leo Buscaglia when

---

45   bell hooks, *All About Love* (New York, HarperCollins, 2000), xxvi (Introduction).

he explains why this is such a difficult problem: Love can't be forced because, by its nature, it is a learned phenomenon and an emotional reaction. It is a response to a learned group of stimuli and behaviors that is dependent upon interaction with others, or a "dynamic interaction." Buscaglia believes that one does not "fall in or out of" love but instead learns to react to specific stimuli in a particular way and to a certain degree, and this reaction is the "visible index" of love. He also contends that one "grows in love." The more we learn, the more opportunities we find to change behavioral responses and thus our ability to love. Like Fromm and hooks, Buscaglia believes that if you have love, you can give it. If you don't have it, you don't have it to give. And if we wish to know love, we must live love, in action. As he puts it, "Thoughts, readings and discourses on love are of value only as they present questions to be acted upon."[46]

This idea that humans are not born knowing but must learn how to love has spawned an entire industry devoted to studying, researching, teaching, and advising, notably *Getting the Love You Want* and *Keeping the Love You Find* (two books by Dr. Harville Hendrix, noted self-help author). Thomas Lewis and his coauthors observe that the sheer volume and variety of self-help books testifies to the voracious appetite that they feed and the inability to satisfy it.[47]

The sense of satisfaction and relief felt after overcoming the difficulties and finding love is best expressed by the classic and beautiful song "At Last," written by Mack Gordon and Harry Warren and popularized by singer Etta James:

---

46   Leo Buscaglia, *Love, What life is All About* (New York: Random House Publishing Group, 1972), 63.
47   Thomas Lewis, Fari Amini, and Richard Lannon, *A General Theory of Love* (New York, Random House, 2000), 118.

At last
My love has come along
My lonely days are over
And life is like a lovely song

At last
The skies above are blue
My heart's wrapped up in clover
Ever since the night I looked at you

I found a dream that I could speak to
A dream to call my own
I found a thrill to press my cheek to
A thrill like I have never known

Oh when you smile, when you smile at me
That's how the spell was cast
And now here we are in heaven
I found my love at last

These lyrics vividly illustrate a state to which most of us seem to aspire and in which we all feel blissful once we achieve it.

Next comes the fun, sex and love, and the relationship benefits and pitfalls between them.

CHAPTER 5

Sex and Love

I want to kiss you all over
And over again
I want to kiss you all over
'Til the night closes in
'Til the night closes in

No one else can ever make me
Feel the way you do
Oh, so keep on loving me, baby
And I'll keep loving you
It's easy to see
When something's right or something's wrong

So stay with me, baby, and hold me all night long
Show me, show me everything you do
'Cause, baby, no one does it quite like you
I love you, need you, oh, babe

("Kiss You All Over" by Exile, 1978)

There can be no discussion of love without addressing the connection between love and sex. We can all agree that engaging in the act of sex does not mean the partners are in love. This is why prostitution is the oldest profession and pornography a multibillion-dollar industry. But sex between two people in love can be one of the greatest feelings of pleasure and completeness in the human experience. The union of the emotional state of love and the physical act of sexual intercourse can be sublime.

Ethel Person explains that the simultaneous expression of emotional and sexual union is one of few uniquely human experiences. She describes the "concordance" of sex and love as allowing the release of the tension between the mind and the body, through which the "individual transcends the body and escapes, if only momentarily, from his dual nature and from his aloneness."[48] For her, sex is the culmination of the goal of love, which is to overcome separateness and merge with the beloved. Love's purpose is to connect emotionally with the other, and sexual intercourse is the vehicle for the physical act that unites this emotional longing with physical, lustful desire. Achieving orgasm with the one you love is the result of this act and accomplishes that unity, even if only for a short time.

The French term for sexual climax is *la petite mort*, which means "the little death." Maryanne Fisher explains that the French equate orgasm with a heightened spiritual experience similar to death, in the sense that in death, humans surrender their very essence, and in intercourse two people in love surrender their individuality to one another as they physically unite their bodies and hearts. Fisher and her coauthor agree with Person that this kind of sexual union is one of the greatest pleasures of human existence.[49] So how does one achieve this blissful state? Interestingly, it can happen regardless of whether two people have a sexual relationship that *develops into* an emotional one or emotional bonds *precede* the sexual activity. In either case, when the emotional component is added to the physical act, the attachment is further deepened. There is no one way to reach this spiritual union that is so special and distinctly human.

48   Ethel Spector Person, *Dreams of Love and Fateful Encounters: The Power of Romantic Passion* (Ontario, Canada: W.W. Norton, 1988), 81.
49   Ibid.

One thing is certain, however: good sex requires chemistry. Stephen Mitchell's clinical experience shows us that, much like falling in love, chemistry can't be forced, and doing so will likely result in dashed expectations or worse, alienation rather than intimacy. Orgasm for orgasm's sake does not build or enhance a relationship. Because signs of female arousal and orgasm are more subtle than they are in males, the female's failure to achieve orgasm can create doubt in the male about his performance, and this, in turn, can infuse tension into the sexual aspect of a relationship. Is it moving forward or backward? Unstimulating sex can be the result of a stalled relationship, or it can signal the absence of chemistry or inadequate emotional attachment. Mitchell asserts that the risks of sexual passion arise from the belief that "because it is never simply a biological, reflexive action but always partially an act of imagination, sexuality . . . can never be fixed and wholly predictable. In this sense, there is always an unknown, an otherness in the experience of sexuality in both one's partner and in oneself. This unknown and unknowable dimension of sexual passion contributes both to its excitement and its risks."[50]

As a result of this unpredictability, knowing when to make "the move" toward sexual intercourse can be filled with uncertainty. If your relationship doesn't begin with love at first sight, where neither of you can wait to jump into the sack together, but instead proceeds more cautiously, the topic of sex and when to engage in it can be a delicate issue. If you seem too eager, it could suggest that you are only interested in a "hookup." On the other hand, not showing an interest in the physical aspect of your budding relationship could cause the other to wonder if you are interested or whether he/she is attractive enough for you. Physical contact such as kissing, caressing, and fondling, as well as staring into your partner's eyes, will hopefully convey that you are anxious to engage in further, more erotic physical contact.

According to Fisher and Costello, some dating coaches advise that waiting to raise the issue might be preferable to pursuing it and forcing

---

50   Stephen A. Mitchell, *Can Love Last, The Fate of Romance Over Time* (New York, W.W. Norton & Company,2002), 79.

the end game too soon.[51] This is obviously a deeply personal decision between the two of you, but in my opinion, this decision should be guided by the woman's behavior. When it comes to sex, women today are more confident and self-assured than society allowed them to be in the past, and many will express in no uncertain terms, either physically or verbally, that they are ready for that significant step. The added benefit of this path is that the woman will be more confident that the man's primary motivation during the dating phase was not merely sex but love, and intercourse will simply be the natural next step for both of you to express these deeper feelings.

When Susan and I started dating, I made a conscious decision not to raise the idea of sleeping together. When I dropped her off at her apartment after a date, we kissed and hugged, and as the dates increased, this intimate contact went on for longer and longer each time. But it was not until after we had been seeing each other for nearly a month, when she came out to the beach house for a weekend (where she stayed in her own bedroom), that the topic came up. We were on the beach, having an evening picnic as the sun was setting, and she turned to me without warning and said softly, "I think it's time." I stopped eating the chicken leg I had in my hand, leaned over, kissed her, and immediately packed up and had her in the car headed home before she could change her mind! After that first time, our sexual appetites fueled the fire of our love, and the second bedroom at the beach house went unused for the rest of the summer.

Talking about sex and making sure that you're both on the same page is critical, both to building a new relationship and to restarting one in which desire has waned. Fisher and Costello assert that sex can be a restorative and healing balm to a troubled relationship, but you must discuss it as a couple. The discussion may be about your sexual likes and dislikes, about time and place, or about frequency, but whatever the topic, it is vital to listen, understand, and respect the

---

51   Maryanne Fisher and Victoria Costello, *The Complete Idiot's Guide to the Chemistry of Love* (New York, Penguin Group, 2010), 81.

other's wishes and needs. It does not aid the relationship when one partner complains, "I told you I don't like it when you do that." Nor does it strengthen bonds when one person simply appeases the other and suffers in silence, enduring behavior that is not enjoyable. This can breed resentment at your partner's insensitivity.

Discussions about sex can also shed light on the overall relationship. If you are sensitive to and respectful of your partner's likes and dislikes in the bedroom, chances are you will be equally sensitive to issues unrelated to sex. Fisher and Costello warn that "honest conversation about sexual expression is imperative if you want sex to be a healing element in your relationship. Too many couples are afraid to talk about sex, and the results are assumptions and expectations that, if not discussed, will harm the relationship. It becomes essential that if you are sexual, you must also be able to give voice to your sexual needs, desires and wishes and you must listen to your partner in a receptive, loving way."[52]

Discussion about sex in a long-term relationship should focus on how to keep it interesting and passionate. Mitchell warns that it is that "knowing" of your partner that can kill romantic passion. We discussed earlier the concept that habituation can kill desire.

When the unknown becomes known, destabilization of the commitment can occur. An element of mystery and spontaneity must exist to sustain romantic relationships. Mitchell advises that "in order for romantic involvements to remain vital and robust over time, it is crucial that the commitment not be so rigid as to override spontaneity and that spontaneity not be so rigid as to preclude commitment." The trick is to keep the passion (sex) interesting.[53] Person refers to periodic intervals of intensity that keep sex interesting as "love attacks," which can sustain interest in and commitment to the other person, allowing them to achieve the merging of emotions and sexual experience discussed in the opening of this chapter. She cites German sociologist

---

52   Ibid., 58.
53   Stephen A. Mitchell, *Can Love Last, The Fate of Romance Over Time* (New York: W.W. Norton & Company, 2002), 49, 199.

and philosopher Georg Simmel, who believed that a long-term, passionate relationship is possible when the "capacity for passionate engagement remains alive and emerges intermittently."[54]

While spontaneity is important, scheduled lovemaking can be equally rewarding. Fisher and Costello advise setting aside "alone time," preferably once a week, solely for the purpose of intimacy. To rekindle lost passion, one technique is to set a date to make love and stick to it. Instead of jumping right into bed, many sex therapists advise taking it slowly. Talk about your shared goal to rejuvenate the passion you once had and that you want to revive it. Touch each other playfully, kiss and hug, and reassure your partner that there is no requirement that you engage in sex, only that you begin to rekindle the passion. Talk about the history of your relationship and how you clawed at each other years ago. Scientifically speaking, sexual stimulation is not only a physical reaction but also occurs in the brain. Even orgasm occurs in the brain, a scientific fact not widely known. For example, research shows that even a castrated man can achieve orgasm through stimulation of another part of his body, creating an erogenous zone. So even talking about sex can stimulate areas of the brain that control sexual arousal. Thus, a thoughtful approach to this effort can result in the return of passion.[55]

So, if there is so much more to the concept of love than just sex, why is all this talk of sex so important? The truth is that sensual gratification, in varying degrees, is always a part of love. Leo Buscaglia writes, "Love touches, love fondles, love hugs, love kisses and it is difficult to think of a situation involving romantic love where one loves deeply without the desire for some sexual gratification."[56] As the years pass, it is important for both parties to be motivated to continue the effort to maintain sexual contact. This is part of what helps keep the bonds of love strong and unbreakable.

---

54   Ethel Spector Person, *Dreams of Love and Fateful Encounters: The Power of Romantic Passion* (Ontario, Canada: W.W. Norton, 1988), 329.

55   Maryanne Fisher and Victoria Costello, *The Complete Idiot's Guide to the Chemistry of Love* (New York: Penguin Group, 2010), 84–86.

56   Ibid., 131.

CHAPTER 6

The Science of Love

If love is a drug
my chemist doesn't have it.
Where can I find some?

("Bottled Love Haiku" © Brian Morton 2014)

This chapter examines the science that is the foundation for much of what we discuss throughout this book and provides evidence for the principles espoused and observations made about love. Why is science relevant to our goal? Well, the more I delved into the physiological aspects—i.e., brain functions, chemical reactions, etc.—that underlie the experience of falling, being, and remaining in love, the more I learned that science could shed light on what we feel in our hearts. It is always valuable to have insight into why we behave the way we do and what influences our behavior toward our beloved. Knowledge is power, as they say, and though you will learn that some of the physiology of love may be out of our direct control, the awareness of everything that drives our feelings and emotions can aid us in understanding and thus influencing our interactions with our partners or potential partners.

Following is a review of biological, neuropsychological, chemical, anatomical, and evolutionary literature of the science underlying the process of falling in love, what emotions and feelings are, what is happening in your brain when you are in love, and the evolutionary factors around mate selection. I find it fascinating, but if you are not interested in the science aspect of love, skimming this chapter will not detract from the overall value of the book or its use in providing guidance on how to develop a loving relationship. However, if you'd like a broader understanding of the complexity of love and relationships and the physiology of it all, please enjoy.

THE BRAIN'S VIEW OF LOVE

We begin our scientific exploration in the mind, with research that utilizes functional MRI (fMRI) to examine areas of the brain that are engaged in the process of love. An fMRI measures brain activity by detecting changes associated with blood flow, because when an area of the brain is in use, there is increased blood flow to that region. In research published in the *Journal of Sexual Medicine*, Stephanie Ortigue and her colleagues examined the cortical networks involved when one is "in love," focusing on the three different types of love: passionate, companionate, and unconditional. She defines passionate love as "a state of intense longing for union with another that is characterized by a motivated and goal-directed mental state"; companionate love is the love felt in a friendship; and unconditional, or maternal love, is love of family or for those with intellectual disabilities.

Ortigue and her colleagues conducted their research by comparing fMRI neuroimaging results of people in passionate love with those of unconditional love to determine if there was a distinct neural basis for passionate love. They discovered a common element throughout the three types of love, namely activity in the reward center of the brain that involves dopamine and oxytocin receptors. This "dopaminergic system" mediates functions that are important for goal-directed motivational reward and pair-bonding, i.e. falling in love.[57] The researchers observed that this finding agrees with theories

---

57   Stephanie Ortigue, Francesco Bianchi-Demichelli, Nisa Patel, Chris Frum, and Lewis W. James, "Neuroimaging of Love: fMRI Meta-Analysis Evidence Toward New Perspectives in Sexual Medicine," *Journal of Sexual Medicine* 7, (2010): 3541–3552.

that define love as a central motivation for pair-bonding in human beings. However, based upon the different areas of the brain that "lit up" on fMRI, areas known as the caudate nucleus and putamen, which are also part of the dopaminergic system, Ortigue and her colleagues differentiate passionate love from the other two types, explaining that passionate love is more than a basic emotion but is instead a complex positive emotion that is reward based and goal directed toward a specific partner.

Dr. Helen Fisher reached the same conclusions when she examined the brains of people who reported being deeply in love. Using fMRI with young lovers, she found that another part of this same dopamine system (ventral tegmental area) lit up during her experiments. She points out that this is the area that actually makes dopamine and sends it out to other areas of the brain. This particular area generates wanting, seeking, craving, energy, focus, and motivation. Fisher's colleagues working in China obtained identical results, proving that this is a natural human response and is not defined by variables such as culture or location.[58]

Fisher and her researchers also found that one of the areas of the brain, the nucleus accumbens, which is fueled by dopamine and is associated with all types of addiction, such as cocaine, heroin, nicotine, alcohol, gambling, sex, and food, was activated on fMRI of people "in love." In other words, the drive to obsess about, crave, and want the lover during the height of the initial romantic period reads the same on fMRI as heroin addiction! You are figuratively and literally addicted to your partner.[59]

To appreciate how little conscious control we have over the beginnings of the process of love and the initiation of sexual desire, we must look at the evolutionary anatomy of the brain. Thomas Lewis and his coauthors discuss the Triune Brain theory, originally

---

58   Helen Fisher, *Anatomy of Love: A Natural History of Mating, Marriage, and Why We Stray* (New York, W.W. Norton & Company, Inc., 2016), 38–39.
59   Ibid., 39.

coined in 1952 by neuroscientist Paul MacLean, which tells us that the human brain is a compilation of the remnants of three brains: the reptilian, the limbic, and the neocortical, all of which evolved at different times over hundreds of thousands of years.[60]

The reptilian brain is the original and oldest. It controls most of our involuntary functions, such as breathing, modulation of blood-sodium content, heartbeat, swallowing, and visual tracking. This is where the startle center is, otherwise known as fight or flight. But this center has nothing to do with who we are, what sets us apart from other animals, or the source of our emotions. In other words, lizards, as far as we know, don't have emotions.

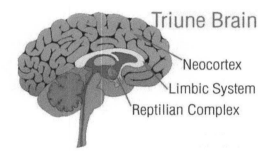

As mammals split off from this reptilian branch, a new neural structure evolved, known as the limbic brain, which is generally considered to be the physical source of emotions. This split also altered the mechanics of reproduction from laying eggs to giving birth to live babies, a development that included nurturing those offspring. As we know today, mammals form close-knit groups, or families, who take care of one another. Mammals also communicate with their offspring and play with one another. This is distinct from an iguana, for example, which hatches from an egg and lives largely in solitude or at most with a mate. Play, nurturance, social communion, and communication all have their origins in the limbic system.

---

60   Thomas Lewis, Fari Amini, and Richard Lannon, *A General Theory of Love* (New York: Random House, 2000), 20–34.

Finally, we have the neocortex, the most evolved part of the brain, which includes the frontal lobes. From here, the motor cortex produces amazing feats of coordination that underlie the simplest tasks of physical movement. Picking up a glass, for instance, requires the firing of thousands of neurons to work in concert with millions of tiny muscle fibers. Even more fascinating is that experiments conducted by physiology researcher Benjamin Libet showed that there is a "readiness wave," or a measurable electrophysiologic neural potential, which begins a hundred milliseconds *before* the conscious decision is appreciated.[61] The conscious decision to move occurs after the readiness wave has already passed. What we think was our initial decision to move is really an afterthought! This forces us to ask what is really happening when we realize we're attracted to someone. Unconscious activity occurs before the conscious mind recognizes the attraction. Where does that emanate from? The following discussion shows that science does not yet have all the answers.

EMOTIONS AND FEELINGS IN LOVE

It is important to appreciate the complexity of the influence that emotions, the origins of which we may be unaware, have on our conduct and on love in particular. Thomas Lewis and his coauthors explain that "the swirling interactions of humanity's three brains, like the shuttling of cups in a shell game, deftly disguise the rules of emotional life and the nature of love. Because people are most aware of the verbal, rational part of their brains, they assume that every part of their mind should be amenable to the pressure of argument and will. Not so. Words, good ideas, and logic mean nothing to at least two

---

61   Benjamin Libet, "Neural Time Factors in Conscious and Unconscious Mental Functions," *Toward a Science of Consciousness, First Discussion and Debates*, edited by R. Hameroff, A.W. Kaszniak, and A. Scot, (Cambridge MA: MIT Press, 1996): 337–347.

brains out of three. Much of one's mind does not take orders."[62] Brain researchers estimate that more than 95 percent of what the brain does is below consciousness, and yet it shapes conscious thought.[63] David Franks writes about the neuroscience of emotions and sheds light on this point by supplying the characterization that "any single second of consciousness is the smallest iceberg tip in an infinite sea of involuntary synaptic processes sealed away from awareness."[64]

Lewis and colleagues clarify the significance of this realization: "A person cannot direct his emotional life in the way he bids his motor system to reach for a cup. He cannot direct himself to want the right thing, *love* the right person, be happy after a disappointment, or even be happy in happy times. People lack this capacity not through a deficiency of discipline but because the jurisdiction of will is limited to the latest brain and to those functions within its purview. Emotional life can be influenced, but it cannot be commanded."[65] For Lewis and his coauthors, love does not begin with a thought but rather with feelings, and these feelings originate in a place where the intellectual part of the brain holds no sway. This raises the question alluded to by Libet above: "Who is driving the train?"

In this context, then, it is important to understand the difference between emotions and feelings. In *The Psychology of Emotions*, research psychologist Carroll Izard says, "An emotion is experienced as a feeling that motivates, organizes, and guides perception, thought, and action." Izard characterizes emotions as "positive or negative evaluative states with physiological, neurological and cognitive

---

62   Thomas Lewis, Fari Amini, and Richard Lannon, *A General Theory of Love* (New York: Random House 2000), 33.
63   Michael S. Gazzaniga, *The Mind's Past* (Oakland, CA: University of California Press, 1998), 21; George Lakoff and Mark Johnson, *Philosophy in the Flesh: The Embodied Mind and its Challenge to Western Thought* (New York: Basic Books, 1999), 10–11.
64   David Franks, *The Handbook of the Sociology of Emotions*, Volume II, ed. Jan E. Stets and Jonathan H. Turner (New York: Springer Science & Business Media, LLC, 2006), 51.
65   Thomas Lewis, Fari Amini, and Richard Lannon, *A General Theory of Love* (New York: Random House, 2000), 33.

components. They are internal states of the human organism, reflecting the organism's response to external stimuli."[66] They are usually involuntary. Neuroscientist Antonio Damasio tells us that "emotions engage heart rates, blood pressure, skin conductance and endocrine responses." He explains that emotions are *objective and public*, occurring (and therefore able to be seen) in the face, posture, voice, and specific behaviors of a person. The subject is unaware of most of these emotional processes.[67]

Feelings, on the other hand, as Damasio explains, are *private and subjective*, and are the mental states that accompany changes in the body's physical state. They are a conscious reaction to emotions. No one can observe your feelings, nor can you observe a feeling in someone else. But many aspects of emotions are patently observable to others. Damasio recognizes that there are positive and negative emotions.[68] Thomas Lewis and his colleagues identify negative ones such as fear, disgust, anger, jealousy, contempt, pride, guilt, shame, and humiliation.[69] Emotional researcher Paul Ekman identifies positive ones such as enjoyment, amusement, relief, satisfaction, contentment, pride in achievement, joy, and surprise, among others.[70]

To help us better appreciate the distinction between emotions and feelings, neuroscientist Joseph LeDoux explains that humans utilize the tool of language to differentiate between the emotions of fear, anxiety, terror, and apprehension. But he tells us that "none of these words would have any point if it were not for the existence of an underlying emotion system that generates the brain states and bodily expressions to which these words apply." These brain states and

---

66   Carroll Izard, *The Psychology of Emotions* (New York: Plenum Press, 1991), 14–15.
67   Antonio Damasio, *Looking for Spinoza: Joy, Sorrow and the Feeling Brain:* New York: Harcourt Brace, 2003), 28.
68   Antonio Damasio, *A Second Chance for Emotion, Cognitive Neuroscience of Emotion*, ed. Richard Lane and Lynn Nadel (New York: Oxford Univ. Press, 2000), 285.
69   Thomas Lewis, Fari Amini, and Richard Lannon, *A General Theory of Love* (New York: Random House, 2000), 41–42.
70   Paul Ekman, "An Argument for Basic Emotions," *Cognition and Emotions*, Vol 6:3–4 (1992): 169–200.

bodily responses are the fundamental facts of an emotion, and the conscious feelings related to those emotions are the "frills that have added icing to the emotional cake."[71] In other words, neuroscience shows that the underlying processes that cause these feelings are emotions. We *feel* our emotions, but emotions cause those feelings.

In discussing an emotion's capacity to precede and cause a particular line of thought, David Franks references Douglas Massey, professor of sociology at the Woodrow Wilson School of Public and International Affairs at Princeton, who says, "Because of our evolutionary history and cognitive structure . . . unconscious emotional thoughts will precede and strongly influence our rational decisions. Thus, our much-valued rationality is really more tenuous than we humans would like to believe, and it probably plays a smaller role in human affairs than prevailing theories of rational choice would have it."[72] LeDoux also believes that emotions have a powerful influence over cognitive processing. Attention, perception, memory, decision-making, and the conditions that follow each are all influenced by emotional states because emotional arousal organizes and coordinates brain activity.[73]

WHAT *IS* LOVE, REALLY?

I have discussed the difference between emotions and feelings in an attempt to isolate the origin of love. But as to whether or not love itself is even an emotion, a debate currently rages between emotional theorists (generally neuroscientists) on the one hand and psychologists and sociologists on the other. The neuroscientists who suggest that love is not an emotion argue that (1) unlike the basic emotions of

---

71   David Franks, *The Handbook of the Sociology of Emotions*, Volume II, ed. Jan E. Stets and Jonathan H. Turner (New York: Springer Science & Business Media, LLC, 2006), 53.

72   Ibid., 39.

73   Joseph LeDoux, "Cognitive–Emotional Interactions: Listen to the Brain," *Cognitive Neuroscience of Emotion*, ed. Richard Lane and Lynn Nadel (New York: Oxford University Press, 2000): 129-155.

anger, disgust, fear, joy, sadness, and surprise, there is no distinctive universal facial expression associated with the state of love; (2) love is an attitude, a sentiment, a culturally constructed emotional syndrome that requires an object and therefore doesn't exist in a vacuum. It is actually a mixture of several other emotions, such as joy and anxiety; (3) it is a goal-oriented motivational state in which the goal is to preserve and promote the well-being of the object of love, which resembles other basic drives such as hunger, thirst, and sleep.[74] Proponents of this view find support in the results of the fMRIs discussed earlier, which revealed that when pictures of the beloved are viewed, the areas of the brain that are activated are those associated with the motivation to obtain rewards (the dopaminergic reward system). Interestingly, these same areas lead to suppression of both negative emotions and the critical assessment of other people. This could be the physical source of the expression "Love is blind."

The other side of the debate is generally supported by psychologists and sociologists, who consider love to be one of the primary emotions, particularly if one focuses on the short-term moments of love, or "love surges," rather than long-term, committed love. They point to substantial evidence that shows that romantic love exists universally across cultures, historical time, and all age groups. They also cite research that suggests that there are nonverbal signs of love that reveal its origin as an emotion, such as soft and tender facial expressions, hugging, kissing, and mutual gazing. A photo of Susan and me gazing into each other's eyes certainly supports this theory of love as an emotion (see photo below). But to add to our confusion, supporters of this view reference the same fMRI results cited by the opposition, because they show that the areas of the brain that are activated when shown a photo of the beloved are associated with euphoria. This reaction suggests that the individual is undergoing an

---

74   Diane H. Felmlee and Susan Sprecher, *The Handbook of the Sociology of Emotions*, Vol. II, ed. Jan E. Stets and Jonathan H. Turner (New York: Springer Science & Business Media, LLC, 2006), 391.

emotional response, not just a motivational one. Finally, this side of the debate goes on to argue that a motivational component to love does not preclude it from being an emotion. For example, the universally accepted emotion of fear, in which an individual may be motivated to flee a threatening situation, does not eliminate fear from being an emotion. Likewise, love being a motivating factor to engage in certain conduct toward another does not eliminate it from being an emotion.

Perhaps there will never be a conclusive answer to this interesting question. Diane Felmlee and Susan Sprecher note that "for some it seems as if the scientific study of love represents an oxymoron." They wonder whether anything scientists have said about love has not been better expressed by Shakespeare, Emily Dickinson, Monet, or even The Beatles. They conclude that "when the dust settles on the scholarship we have reviewed here, love still remains a mystery."[75]

THE PHYSIOLOGY OF LOVE

Regardless of our collective inability to firmly pinpoint the origin of love, it is clear that love can be expressed in nonverbal communication between two people. To explain this phenomenon, Thomas Lewis and his colleagues, in *A General Theory of Love,* coined the term *limbic resonance,* which occurs when the limbic system of the brain detects and analyzes the internal state of another mammal. The authors explain that "emotionality is the social sense organ of limbic creatures. . . . [It] enables a mammal to sense the inner states and the motives of the mammals around him." The individual can then adjust its own physiology to match the situation, a change that is sensed by the other, who can, in turn, adjust. This is *"limbic resonance*—a symphony of mutual exchange and internal adaptation whereby two mammals become attuned to each other's inner states." Eye contact, for example, causes two nervous systems to "achieve a palpable

---

75   Ibid., 406.

and intimate apposition."[76] *Limbic resonance* is the door to this "communal connection" and supplies the wordless communication we see all around us but take for granted, such as what happens between mother and infant, a boy and his dog, or lovers holding hands and gazing into each other's eyes. This connection occurs much like other noiseless functions of organs such as the liver or kidneys, smoothly and continuously, without our notice.

Below is a photo of limbic resonance occurring between Susan and me. Six months into our relationship, I took Susan to the famous Rainbow Room restaurant for her birthday, where we were photographed on the dance floor. Anyone viewing this photo could see that our brains were connecting and, not coincidently, that we were deeply in love at the time.

This particular feature of mammalian brain function explains why feelings are contagious. We perceive what the other person is feeling and join them, whether they are our lover or simply others around us. If the other person is sad, we become quiet and withdrawn. If the person is happy, it becomes contagious, and we join them in their reverie. According to Lewis and his coauthors, the physiology of this interaction is real.

---

76   Thomas Lewis, Fari Amini, and Richard Lannon, *A General Theory of Love* (New York: Random House, 2000), 63.

BACK TO CHEMISTRY

The topic of the science behind love would not be complete without a discussion of chemistry, which is the foundation of brain function mediating all the emotions and feelings that drive this complicated condition that we call love. While brain chemistry is complex, evolutionary psychologist Maryanne Fisher and her coauthor, Victoria Costello, attempt to put it into terms we can comprehend. They explain that there are different categories of chemicals in the body that are involved in the process of love.[77]

Hormones, which underlie our emotional states, are the first category. The hormone oxytocin is a protein that courses through both the blood and nervous system, and because it operates through both of these pathways, it has a tremendous effect on the chemistry of love. Oxytocin reduces stress and anxiety and aids in relaxation. It is initiated by touch, so simply holding hands with your lover will increase oxytocin levels. This is why hugging or holding the hands of those in distress is comforting to them. During the process of "falling in love," merely thinking about the object of our love raises these levels and makes us feel better.

The hormone testosterone is produced in both men and women and is behind assertiveness and aggression, whether in sports, business, war, or sex. It is also the chemical that fuels "lust." Estrogen, also found in both men and women, produces feelings of calmness and contentment. There are three varieties in women, all of which have different functions at different stages of life. Men have only one type of estrogen, but it can increase the bonding effect of oxytocin and can also affect the desire to "cuddle," which feels good.

Vasopressin increases attention and enhances memory and the ability to regulate emotions. It also modulates the impact of testosterone on male sexual behavior, to keep that lust in check, so to speak.

---

77   Maryanne Fisher and Victoria Costello, *The Complete Idiot's Guide to the Chemistry of Love* (New York: Penguin Group, 2010), 29–36.

Endorphins increase feelings of well-being and typically have the greatest influence *after* the infatuate and romantic stages of a relationship, because they carry calming properties that allow you to engage in activities together and pay less attention to those hormones that fuel lust and encourage you to tear each other's clothes off!

Another category of chemicals is neurotransmitters, which carry the electrical impulses between the synapses, the structures that are responsible for brain communication. The most important neurotransmitter that pertains to this particular discussion is dopamine, which is associated with all types of pleasure. Not only does it bring instant pleasure but it promotes the anticipation of pleasure to come in the future, which is why it plays a role in all types of addiction. It has a central role in the brain's "reward system" and is the fast-track-delivery messenger of joy, ecstasy, and delight, which is the short-lived dopamine "rush" that we hear about, as opposed to the longer-term happiness that is mediated by oxytocin. Lust is triggered by dopamine, which activates testosterone and is released at orgasm.

Serotonin, another neurotransmitter, is a natural antidepressant and mood elevator. Serotonin levels rise when you're in love but fall when you're depressed. A neurotransmitter called phenylethylamine (PEA) is a natural amphetamine that fluctuates according to your thoughts, feelings, and experiences. It is PEA that causes that giddiness and excitement during the "falling" stage of love. PEA is also believed to be the chemical responsible for "love at first sight" because it floods the brain during initial attraction. It, too, is released during orgasm, thus contributing to the good feeling and causing us to want more.

Finally, there is norepinephrine, a neurotransmitter that is a natural stimulant. Central to the fight-or-flight response to perceived danger, this chemical puts the body on alert in a dangerous situation or revs up the senses during an exciting or engaging one, as in the initial stages of attraction.

Helen Fisher summarizes the influence that these chemicals have at various stages in the development of love as follows: "Lust is primarily associated with testosterone in both men and women; romantic love is linked with dopamine, norepinephrine and serotonin; and feelings of deep attachment are mediated by oxytocin and vasopressin."[78] As discussed earlier, she cites research that shows that the reward system in the brains of those who report being in love activates on an fMRI in the same way as addicts who have ingested cocaine or opioids. So those who are intensely and happily in love show on an fMRI as being addicted to their beloved. Fisher's research partner, Lucy Brown, also proposed that romantic love is a natural addiction, a normal state that can be experienced by almost all human beings. Even when one partner is cast aside by the other, the feeling of addiction continues as we remain chemically attached to the other; the craving for them is a tangible, physical loss. The sudden lack of dopamine is similar to a physical withdrawal from drugs.

Learning about the chemicals involved in the process of love can help us appreciate that it is a process influenced by factors that are often beyond our control. All of these hormones and neurotransmitters act together during the initial stage of attraction and also when falling and staying in love. These involuntary stimulants affect your response when meeting someone new or seeing someone you already know in a new light and discovering something you hadn't previously noticed about them. They contribute to that unconscious influence on your emotions that can then be regulated by the neocortex, the thinking part of your brain.

EVOLUTIONARY LOVE STRATEGIES

Now let's move beyond chemicals and talk about another scientific factor that influences the process of falling in love, as well as our ability to hold on to our mate. Maryanne Fisher, noted feminist and evolutionary biologist, has written extensively about the evolutionary

---

78   Helen Fisher, *Anatomy of Love: A Natural History of Mating, Marriage, and Why We Stray* (New York: W.W. Norton & Company, Inc., 2016), 151.

forces that influence landing a mate and keeping him/her. She explains that the most current research on this topic can be traced back to Charles Darwin's theory of evolution, specifically sexual selection, in which characteristics evolve that enable individuals to gain advantage over same-sex competitors. This evolution of characteristics applies to both men and women because the research shows that it helps them achieve access to and retention of mates.[79] In the male-dominated field of biological psychology, women have historically been viewed as having a relatively passive place in the evolutionary process. Fisher asserts, however, that there is no doubt that women compete against one another for attractive mates and says that "viewing women as competitive therefore reflects a shift towards perceiving women as active agents." Her work and that of other feminist academics has changed the focus of prior research, which had been about what happens *to* women, and instead focuses on how women's behavior influences human evolution.[80] She explains that research over the past twenty years demonstrates that advances in methodology and research design have provided empirical evidence of women's subtle and covert competition with other women.[81] She tells us that researchers today are drawing attention to the fact that "we must dispel the negativity surrounding, or placement of values on, women's competition and instead focus on the evolutionary basis of this activity."[82]

In Fisher's chapter, which includes research by some fifty-three female evolutionary psychologists, she concludes, "What is abundantly clear is that women do compete (typically with each other) and that the form of this competition is often indirect, covert and circuitous."[83] Fisher also anticipates that the cultural shift to more

---

79   Ibid., 21.
80   Maryanne Fisher, Editor, *The Oxford Handbook of Women and Competition* (New York: Oxford Univ. Press, 2017), 4.
81   Ibid., 5.
82   Ibid., 20.
83   Ibid., 6.

egalitarian gender roles will result in less stigma attached to women competing in a direct manner for mates, resources, and status.[84] I have included this science because much of what Fisher's research shows to me now, with the benefit of hindsight, is that Susan engaged in this process in precisely the ways described by the research. I find it fascinating to unknowingly have been on the receiving end of evolutionarily based conduct that achieved what it sought for Susan, namely to obtain and keep a mate. It is interesting to me because I lived it and was the recipient of this behavior without knowing its scientific basis. The scientific knowledge of what influences behavior, in this case evolutionary forces about competition between women, should be of interest to men and women alike.

The discussion that follows is not meant to be a primer on what women should do to achieve the goal set in this book, which is nurturing and extending the relationship with your current partner. It is offered merely to explain the evolutionary process of attracting and keeping a mate. Evolutionary theory tells us that males, to continue the species and enhance the chances of healthy offspring, seek out females who appear fertile, while rejecting those who appear infertile.[85] Over many millennia, men have developed preferences for physical features that will help them to distinguish fertile women accurately and reliably from less fertile women. In fact, Fisher devotes four chapters of research, written by nine evolutionary psychologists, to the importance of physical appearance and how it is integral to female competition for mates. Research shows that the physical indicators valued by men and that suggest fertility are youth, full lips, smooth skin, lustrous hair, and femininity, rather than graying hair and aging skin that has lost its youthful glow. Another reliable indicator of female fertility is a low waist-to-hip ratio, which is the result of full breasts, a small waist, and larger hips.

---

84   Ibid., 4.
85   D. J. DelPriore, M. L. Prokosch, and S. E. Hill, *The Causes and Consequences of Women's Competitive Beautification*, ed. Maryanne L. Fisher, *The Oxford Handbook of Women and Competition* (New York: Oxford Univ. Press, 2017), 58.

And because these physical features are so highly valued by men, and women are evolutionarily programmed to continue the human race, intrasexual competition among women is common, manifesting itself as a battle to be the most desirable to men. This competition can be seen in a variety of activities and behaviors that women utilize to enhance their appearance. Studies show that women put enormous effort into enhancing their appearance to both attract and keep romantic partners. They do this with cosmetics and other beauty products and by displaying or improving physical attractiveness by wearing flattering clothing, maintaining a healthy diet, exercising, and even tanning. Some may feel the need to increase their sexual appeal with a bust-enhancing bra or even plastic surgery. In fact, a study conducted by French psychologist Nicolas Guéguen to determine the effectiveness of such strategies demonstrated that a woman who wore a special bra that allowed her to artificially manipulate the perception of her breast size was approached by more male suitors at a bar as her bust size increased. A second study conducted by Guéguen asked a young woman to stand by the side of a road frequented by hitchhikers and hold out her thumb. As her bust size grew, so did the number of male drivers who stopped to offer her a ride.[86] Yet another study showed that men rated women wearing high-heeled shoes as being considerably more attractive than those wearing flats.[87]

While much of this is not surprising to most of us, the idea that these behaviors are scientifically founded upon evolutionary forces is enlightening. In truth, adorning oneself with attractive clothing and jewelry to lure a mate has been common practice since the beginning of human existence. Archeological evidence has found

---

86   N. Guéguen, "Bust Size and Hitchhiking: A Field Study," *Perceptual and Motor Skills*, 2007;105 (3_suppl): 1294-1298; N. Guéguen, "Women's Bust Size and Men's Courtship Solicitation," *Body Image* 4(4) (January 2007): 386–390.
87   P. Morris, J. White, E. Morrison, and K. Fisher, "High heels as supernormal stimuli: How wearing high heels affects judgements of female attractiveness." *Evolution and Human Behavior* 34 (2013): 176–181.

that women who made the first animal-skin tunics decorated them with rare beads or paint. Unearthed remnants of clothing adorned with beads, embroidery, and dye prove that clothing was used for more than protection. Even in ancient times, clothing had two functions: dress and adornment, or modification of the body. Use of body paint, permanent ink, piercing, and purposeful body scarring have no protective benefit, so the only discernible reason for this type of adornment was to enhance physical appearance in order to display status and/or societal rank to potential mates.

Throughout history, women have used clothing, cosmetics, plastic surgery, or other treatments, such as Botox, to enhance their attractiveness and thus their perceived fertility and desirability. Additional studies cited by DelPriore and her colleagues support the notion that men perceive women with cosmetic enhancement as being more attractive than those without. So even today, when women have made so many advances with regard to equality and independence from men, intrasexual competition is still influenced by evolution, which propels them to continue to make themselves look and feel beautiful and younger in order to attract a desirable mate. We need look no further for evidence than the multibillion-dollar beauty industry.

Even color is a significant factor in attracting a mate. In many species in nature, particularly in our primate relatives, red is a sign of fertility. A female primate's genitals swell and redden when she is ovulating and looking for a mate. In humans, research has shown that the color a woman chooses to wear often depends on whether she is menstruating. Women who are in a "high-fertility" stage will choose red or pink rather than other colors.[88] There is also evidence that women interested in casual sex are more likely to wear red. This is true cross-culturally, in that red has been associated with desire, lust, jealously, and love (consider Cupid and red Valentine hearts,

---

88   Laurel L. Johnsen and Glenn Geher, "Fashion as a Set of Signals in Female Intrasexual Competition," Fisher, Maryanne, Editor, *The Oxford Handbook of Women and Competition* (New York: Oxford Univ. Press, 2016).

for example). Another study showed that men perceived a woman wearing a red blouse more attractive than a woman wearing a blue one and were more likely to ask the woman wearing red on a date and spend money on her. So fashion is clearly a tactic women use to attract men, but there is also competition between women who wear revealing clothing that men perceive as sexy and alluring and women who try to strike a balance between sexy and modest clothing. Men perceive this latter category more favorably in terms of personality, intelligence, and lack of promiscuity.

Throughout my relationship with Susan, I often noticed her efforts to enhance her appearance, though obviously I was not aware of the scientific basis. On our first date, she wore medium-height heels with a loose, flowing dress that fell below the knee but adequately showed off her figure. The dress was red. To me it confidently declared, "I am attractive, conscious about dressing well, want to attract your attention, but I'm not looking for a one-night stand." I got the message. I didn't appreciate it at the time, but this evolutionarily based behavior was intended to attract and keep my attention, because she recognized the psychological importance of the waist-to-bust ratio.

Though I assured Susan at various times throughout our relationship that she didn't have to do anything to keep my interest, she nevertheless made small cosmetic enhancements from time to time and sought out treatments and products that would help her to remain youthful looking. She was attractive and didn't look her age because she took care of her skin with a variety of creams and lotions that kept it smooth and glistening. She had frequent facials, manicures, and pedicures, and regularly went to a hair stylist. After her death, an old friend of hers sent me a picture of Susan as a teenager. I was surprised to see that she had been overweight, which meant that her efforts to become slim had been successful and, to be honest, made her more attractive and appealing as a potential mate. All of this worked on me like a charm. After we'd been dating a month or so, I proposed that we become exclusive so we could find out if it would work between us because, given her looks and brains, I was concerned that she would not be "on the market" for long. Her Darwinian-based behaviors to outcompete other women not only made her an attractive mate but forced my hand to move quickly. Of course, we were both beyond childbearing age, so evolutionary factors regarding fertility were not a driving force, but they nevertheless made her appealing as a potential long-term mate and continued to influence her behavior throughout our relationship.

Susan's attention to her looks did not diminish after she was diagnosed with ovarian cancer. She naturally worried about losing her hair as a result of the chemotherapy treatment. She had had a number of different "cocktails" of medicines but only one caused her to lose her hair. She was mortified and bought wigs, but they were all uncomfortable and hot. Nevertheless, she wore them in public and made up herself as she had always done. She refused to let the cancer get the best of her.

I thought that traveling between the six- to eight-week cycles of treatment would be a beneficial distraction that might lift her spirits. Our first trip after she had lost her hair from the chemo was to Barcelona. At dinner one night, I suggested that she discard the wig, pointing out that we were in a foreign country where she didn't know anyone and where she could be comfortable and less concerned with her appearance. She resisted, but I persisted, and she finally removed her wig. Her hair had partially grown back, though it was very short and gray, but she felt liberated without the wig. She kept it off for the rest of the trip, which made it more enjoyable for her.

Susan had always worn her hair down to her shoulders, but I told her she looked prettiest when she put it up in a French twist because it showed off her beautiful face. When we returned home from that trip, she kept her hair short but colored it her natural blond. She looked fabulous. Her friends all told her she looked better with short hair, so she stuck with it. It made her feel good that she was able to deal with the ravages of the cancer treatment and still look and feel attractive. She would not allow cancer to interfere with her evolutionarily honed desire to look her best for herself and her mate.

In *Evolution's Empress: Darwinian Perspectives on the Nature of Women*, which Maryanne Fisher also edited, research reveals that competition among women is even more sophisticated than it would seem at first glance. Discussed is the idea that females' competition patterns depend on the type of relationship they seek. When seeking a brief interaction, women will compete in ways to advertise their physicality, sexuality, and lack of interest in a commitment, whereas when seeking a long-term partner, they will advertise parenting abilities and fidelity. The research further showed that women who were in pursuit of a long-term relationship highlighted their faithfulness and sexual restrictiveness over their sexual attractiveness. And strategies to attract a mate continue even after the relationship forms, to ensure that the interest of the male is maintained. This explains why Susan made such an effort with her appearance even after we were married and throughout her battle with cancer.

Competition to attract a mate is an evolutionary force equally strong in men as it is in women. In fact, Fisher points out that past research has primarily focused on male intrasexual competition, and it's only recently that attention has been paid to female competition. But clearly, men also engage in a variety of behaviors and intrasexual competition to attract and keep a mate. Just as Susan engaged in competitive conduct with regard to me, I, too, exhibited similar behavior toward her. As most of us know, a basic evolutionary tool that men use to outcompete other men is strength. So when I began staying over at Susan's apartment more frequently, I suggested that we go to the local gym and work out together. Whether consciously or unconsciously, I saw an opportunity to display to her how fit, and therefore virile, I was. Not necessarily subtle but nonetheless effective.

I also made a conscious choice to always dress well, not only while we were dating, but even after we were living together, because I knew that would ward off sloppy or unkempt competitors. Finally, when we first started dating I shared with her difficult legal cases on which I was working, because this conveyed competence and success, which reassured her of potential financial security.

There is little doubt that men also continue competitive behaviors throughout the relationship, because they have a lifelong need to be perceived as strong, protective, competent, and successful. My evolutionary tactics were strength, style, and security. I'm thrilled to say that they worked! Such strategies can help keep a relationship fresh and exciting once it has begun, so we'll discuss some of them in the next chapter.

CHAPTER 7

How to Create and Maintain a Lasting, Loving, Fulfilling Relationship

Young and beautiful
But someday your looks will be gone
When the others turn you off
Who'll be turning you on?
I will, I will, I will
I will be there to share forever
Love will keep us together

("Love Will Keep Us Together" by Neil Sedaka and Howard Greenfield, 1973)

I finished getting dressed, tightening my tie as I walked into our kitchen, where Susan was making breakfast.

"How do you think this tie looks with this shirt?" I asked.

"You look strong but not overbearing. You look great!" she said, offering me encouragement for the day in court. She knew I had to cross-examine an important defense witness that day.

The walls around our little table were filled with framed pictures of the places we'd seen together—the Eiffel Tower, Notre Dame, Sacré-Coeur, cathedrals in Bordeaux and Lyon, and the Leaning

Tower of Pisa. I gazed at the large print of a man having morning coffee at a café while reading the paper. We bought it at a charming hilltop village called Lourmarin in Provence. These memories of our travels comforted us both. They were evidence of the new life we had created for each other.

"We have to figure out what to do for the holidays," Susan said. She was directing the course of the morning's organizational briefing that we enjoyed at breakfast time to plan our respective days.

"Well, the boys have to be with Mary on Christmas Eve, but I think this year, Pete and Alice are with her parents on Christmas. So they can't be here with me for Christmas," I said. I was facing the prospect of not seeing my youngest son over the holidays.

Susan was trying to figure out when she could cook a family meal for all of our kids and get commitments from them to attend. Given the different directions the kids of divorced parents are usually pulled, this wasn't easy.

"Andy will want to see Danny and Lindsay one of those days, so I don't know how we're going to work this out," she responded.

"What? Is Andy celebrating Jewish Christmas with the kids?" I mildly pushed back.

"I always had a big Christmas tree in the house in South Orange, so he got used to it and will want to see them," she explained.

"Well, if he can live with Christmas Eve, we can have everyone here for Christmas minus Pete," I complained.

"I know how we can solve this. There are eight days of Hanukkah, and Andy can take any one with our kids. Your kids won't be doing anything, so we can have a Hanukkah party. That way everyone can be here," my smart wife figured out.

"Right. My kids can't tell me they'll be busy for Hanukkah, although I wouldn't put it past them to try!"

One of the main ingredients to a successful relationship is communication. Susan and I demonstrated our commitment to regular communication through these daily "organizational briefings." Each morning over breakfast, we discussed the upcoming day's activities, what we each had to do, and if we could help each other in any way. These meetings became a habit that showed our respective investment in our relationship by engaging in ongoing communication.

That particular morning was spent figuring out how to deal with our blended family. If either party in a relationship has been married before, there will inevitably be challenges, especially if children are involved. Of course, if the children dislike the new partner, it will be more difficult to maintain a stable relationship.

How to blend families deserves its own book, but if you're faced with this issue, there's no reason you can't aspire for your respective children to be civil toward your partner and their children, particularly during family gatherings. The ideal, of course, is that in the end, the children become friends, but I recommend tempering your expectations, merely aiming for civility. The reality is that when they aren't raised together from a young age under the same roof, it's a lot to expect them to love one another. Removing the unrealistic expectations of creating a perfectly blended "Brady Bunch" will relieve the pressure from you and your partner and will improve your relationship with each other.

Whether or not you have a blended family or struggle with communication, the challenge is how to build on your initial love so that you can preserve an ideal relationship. It doesn't just happen—it requires a commitment from both parties to do the work. Neither Susan nor I had ever read anything about how to build a strong and positive relationship, but we managed to practice most of the things suggested by experts, probably because we had both been married before. We had learned what worked and what didn't. Since we were both in our fifties when we met, we also brought a certain level of maturity and life experience to our relationship. Of course, without that same level of experience, you can read a book like this and learn from the mistakes of the author rather than make them yourself.

The bottom line is that you can't expect your relationship to be harmonious by magic. The fact that love takes work has been repeated again and again by all who have studied and written about it. This is true regardless of who you are, where you are in the relationship, or how strong you think your relationship already is. Communication is just one of many issues that couples need to address.

Suzann and James Pawelski suggest using the power of positive psychology to create and nurture an enduring relationship. James is a professor and director of education in the Positive Psychology Center at the University of Pennsylvania, and Suzann is an author and well-being consultant who specializes in the science of happiness as it relates to relationships and health. In their book, *Happy Together*, the Pawelskis use staying fit as an analogy for the work necessary to achieve a strong relationship. As we all know, becoming and remaining fit and healthy doesn't happen automatically but is the result of hard work and exercise. Sustained efforts and habits are essential.

Both the Pawelskis and Erich Fromm know that to be good at something takes more than simply *wanting* to be good. To master the art of anything, we have to learn the skills necessary to achieve a high level of proficiency. Fromm says that the "art of love" requires discipline, concentration, and patience. A carpenter, for instance, begins as an apprentice, learning how to plane wood. A pianist first learns how to play piano by practicing scales. If a lifelong healthy relationship is your goal, hard work and practicing the rules set forth in this book are essential. But both parties must commit to it.

Maryanne Fisher and her coauthor explain that this commitment includes three essential components: trust, honesty, and effective communication. They characterize trust as the belief that you are *both* there to stay, equally invested in working on issues that could interfere with your relationship. When difficulties arise, your commitment will compel you to do what's necessary to iron things out, especially when temporary feelings might tell you to do otherwise.[89] This commitment to the relationship is mandatory for the development of the trust that you and your partner must have in each other.

---

89   Maryanne Fisher and Victoria Costello, *The Complete Idiot's Guide to the Chemistry of Love* (New York: Penguin Group, 2010), 56.

In *The Road Less Traveled*, M. Scott Peck reinforces the importance of this notion of committing to the relationship: "Whether it be shallow or not, commitment is the foundation, the bedrock of any genuinely loving relationship. Deep commitment does not guarantee the success of the relationship but does more help than any other factor to ensure it."[90]

In *Can Love Last?*, however, psychoanalyst Stephen Mitchell advises that this commitment not be rigid, so that we're merely devoted to the idea of staying together. We need to dedicate ourselves to the process of working out our problems together, even when faced with uncertainty. There will always be differences and problems, but the security of a relationship is built on the process that the parties agree upon.

Mitchell warns that "in order for romantic involvement to remain vital and robust over time, it's crucial that the commitment not be so rigid as to override spontaneity and that the spontaneity not be so rigid as to preclude commitment."[91] Security and predictability are inconsistent with genuine passion for each other, so even though relationships change over time, couples should strive to maintain as much of the passion that brought them together in the first place. Mitchell proposes that "the cultivation of romance in relationships requires two people who are fascinated by the ways in which individually and together they generate forms of life they hope they can count on."[92]

OBJECTIVITY, FAITH, COURAGE, AND TRANSPARENCY

Besides the importance of communication and commitment, there are other important essential rules to help you maintain a successful relationship.

---

90   M. Scott Peck, *The Road Less Traveled: A New Psychology of Love, Traditional Values and Spiritual Growth* (New York: Touchstone, 1978), 140.
91   Stephen A. Mitchell, *Can Love Last, The Fate of Romance Over Time* (New York: W.W. Norton & Company, 2002), 199.
92   Ibid., 199–201.

According to Erich Fromm in *The Art of Loving*, overcoming our narcissism or love of self over all others is the primary challenge to being able to love someone else. To clarify what he means by narcissism, he describes its polar opposite, which is objectivity or the ability to see life as it really is rather than how we'd like it to be. He illustrates his point with an extreme example of an insane person who fails to see the outside world objectively because his only reality is made up of the fears and desires in his own mind.

Naturally, there are degrees of this lack of objectivity, but the bottom line is that we can't love when we have a distorted picture of our love object—a picture that has likely been influenced by our experiences as a child. Fromm offers two examples of archetypes that illustrate failings of objectivity. A man who had an overbearing mother may feel that his freedom is restricted when any woman makes a demand on him. Obviously, he's going to struggle in relationships. Similarly, a woman might believe that men are weak when they don't live up to her knight-in-shining-armor fantasy. As a result, she's going to be disappointed in any relationship.[93]

To be objective, or at least sensitive to situations where we might fail to be objective, we need reason and humility. The goal is seeing the difference between our narcissistically distorted picture of our partner and the reality of who they are, regardless of our own interests, needs, or fears.

Along with objectivity, a second rule that helps us achieve love is the understanding that it requires faith—not religious faith but rational faith that possesses the certainty of our convictions. Faith is indispensable. It means we're certain that the core of the other person's personality, as well as their fundamental attitudes and their love, are reliable and unchangeable. But to achieve this, we must first have faith in ourselves, knowing who we are without being dependent on the approval of others to sustain our sense of self.

---

93   Fromm, Erich, *The Art of Loving*, (New York: Harper & Row, Inc., 1956). 110–111.

Only someone who has faith in himself can have faith in another. We're the only ones who can be certain we'll be the same person in the future as we are in the present, expecting to feel and act toward the person we love in the same way.[94]

If we want to become well versed in the art of love, we also must have courage—the ability to take a risk and the readiness to accept possible pain and disappointment. For Fromm, "To be loved, and to love, needs courage, the courage to judge certain values as of ultimate concern—and to take the jump and stake everything on these values." He summarizes this idea like this: "To love means to commit oneself without guarantee, to give oneself completely in the hope that our love will produce love in the loved person. Love is an act of faith, and whoever is of little faith is also of little love."[95]

When I suggested to Susan that we become exclusive and she agreed, we both took a risk and committed ourselves to the other without guarantee. It took courage because we couldn't know how it would turn out, but we were prepared to accept whatever came.

Of course, as mentioned previously, another critical ingredient that fosters commitment is communication. This means communicating more than just what's on your agenda each day, however. It means communicating your most intimate thoughts and feelings. The end goal is to be as genuinely open and honest as you can be about who you are.

In chapter 2, I mentioned Maryanne Fisher's point that each partner in a relationship is the other's lover, principal companion, sounding board, coparent, and housemate. Those roles require constant and sincere communication, which means being honest with both yourself and your partner. She warns that once dishonesty is rationalized and allowed to enter into the dynamic, the relationship becomes superficial.

This doesn't mean, of course, that you have to confess every stupid or embarrassing thing you've ever done in your life. What if there are

---

94 Ibid., 114.
95 Ibid., 117–118.

things from your past that could be harmful to the relationship and may be better left unsaid? When in doubt about how transparent to be about your past, my advice is to use your best judgment as to what could cause a rift between you or irrevocably damage your partner's opinion of you. Nevertheless, the more open and honest you can be, the better, because that communication will help you both avoid potential problems in the future.

When you discuss past relationships with your current partner, it isn't necessary to discuss every detail. But be transparent about the difficulties you experienced and how you and your partner(s) *both* contributed to the outcome. This can help you build trust between you. If, on the other hand, you place all of the blame on your ex, you immediately raise credibility issues by implying that you were perfect. It takes courage to bring up something that may bring back bad memories, but doing so demonstrates you're committed to making your new relationship work.

For instance, I explained to Susan how working with my second wife, Kathy, contributed to the demise of our relationship. Kathy and I are both competitive people, and during our marriage, we often argued about work issues at home and brought home issues into the office. It wasn't a flattering picture of me, so I didn't enjoy revealing to Susan that I had engaged in behavior that was destructive to my marriage. But I wanted to be as open as possible with her because I knew it was important for her to trust me. I also vowed never to repeat those mistakes.

INNER ACTION

Experts all agree that applying the rules we've discussed in this chapter requires two different types of action. The first comes from within and the second involves what we do for the other. Fromm describes the first type of action as an "inner activity" or "the productive use of one's powers." This activity is "indispensable for the practice of the art of loving." He explains that "love is an activity; if I love, I am in a constant state of active concern with the loved person," which calls for a "constant state of awareness, alertness."[96]

Though not a psychologist like Fromm, feminist author bell hooks discusses this same concept when she advocates for lack of selfishness in a relationship—the "ability to recognize when the other person needs our attention." Hooks quotes psychologist Robert Sternberg, professor of human development at Cornell University and a theorist on intelligence: "If I were asked the single most frequent cause of the destruction of relationships . . . I would say it is selfishness. We live in an age of narcissism, and many people have never learned or have forgotten how to listen to the needs of others. The truth is, if you want to make just one change in yourself that will improve your relationship—literally overnight—it would be to put your partner's interest on an equal footing with your own."[97] This is exactly what Fromm means by inner action.

The Pawelskis offer practical advice on how to put this "inner action" into motion to strengthen the relationship. In *Happy Together*, they explore which of the three potential Rules of Relationships they believe is the best to follow. The first is the Golden Rule: do unto others as you would have them do unto you. In other words, treat the other as you would like to be treated. But the limitation of the Golden Rule is that it directs you to treat others as if they were in your shoes, even though they don't always want the same things you want.

The Pawelskis then critique the second rule, known as the Platinum Rule: treat others as they wish to be treated. That sounds wonderful, but it requires you to know how precisely the other person wishes to be treated, which can be hard to ascertain. On top of this problem, it doesn't help if the other person doesn't know what they want or wants something that may not be beneficial for them. Children want to stay up late, eat candy, and spend inordinate amounts of time playing video

---

96   Ibid. 118–119.
97   bell hooks, *All About Love* (New York: HarperCollins,2000), 162–163.

games. The same can apply to adults. If one person in a relationship is a heavy drinker or smoker, for example, and they want you to accept their destructive behavior or even join them, a codependent relationship rather than a healthy one is most likely to follow.

The best rule, according to the Pawelskis, is what they've coined the Aristotelian Rule, based on the teachings of ancient Greek philosopher Aristotle. To understand why the Pawelskis chose Aristotle's teachings as the foundation of their rule, it's helpful to know more about his philosophy. First, he believed that love is the greatest external good, which refers to attributes outside the person, such as wealth, honor, friends, and political power. Second, he believed that happiness, which he describes as "living well and faring well" or human flourishing, is the aim of human life. Finally, because man is a social animal whose inclination is to live in the company of others, Aristotle offered definitive ideas about friendship and defined three types: (1) self-interested, in which we participate merely to get something out of it; (2) friendship just for the sake of fun; and (3) *real* friendship, which involves appreciating the other person for who they truly are and being generous with that person, sharing experiences and memories. This last type is the one that embodies love.

The best type of love, according to Aristotle, is the one in which two people are attracted to each other because of the good they see in the other. The partners love each other for who they are rather than for what they can get out of the relationship.

The Aristotelian Rule, then, instructs us to treat the other person as *their best self* would have us treat them. In other words, we treat them as that person in their healthiest state would want to be treated. Using this rule, rather than trying to change the other person, we help them build their own character and become a better person by virtue of their positive traits. It stands to reason that if people are attracted to each other because of the good they see in the other, as that good grows, the attraction should also grow, naturally strengthening the relationship with the passage of time. Since each lover is committed to their own growth, the more their partner helps them achieve it, the more they will appreciate the partner. The more both parties' characters improve, the more longlasting and fulfilling their relationship is likely to become. But this state requires "inner action" (Fromm) and lack of selfishness (hooks, Sternberg) to put the interests of our partner on equal footing with our own.

Noted marital researcher John Gottman expresses similar ideas by suggesting that "emotional attunement" to our partner is a fundamental skill needed to sustain relationships. He tells us to "turn toward" our partner with our full attention, express tolerance and understanding, and communicate with empathy in a nondefensive manner. We need to be sensitive to the effect our words can have on the other person.

He coined the acronym ATTUNE, which stands for **A**ttention **T**urning toward **T**olerance, **U**nderstanding, **N**ondefensive responding, and **E**mpathy.[98] This is the mental process we should bring to a relationship, and it builds on Fromm's advice to constantly be alert to our partner.

Psychiatrist and author Ethel Person promoted this concept in more concrete terms. She believed that the most important element of a relationship is that each person be able to tolerate some frustration and feel "satisfied with what is good, not demanding impossible perfection of either the beloved's character or ministration. In this sense, happy love depends in part on temperament, on the ability to look at life on balance. The lover must be able to discount some of the negatives, to blink and look away, to deny and forgive."[99] In other words, as Aristotle advised, accept the person for who they are, finding and loving the good in them.

This means not trying to change someone's personality to satisfy your needs. If someone is shy and introverted, you shouldn't demand

---

98   John Gottman, *The Science of Trust: Emotional Attunement for Couples*, (New York: W.W. Norton, 2011), 176–222.
99   Ethel Spector Person, *Dreams of Love and Fateful Encounters: The Power of Romantic Passion* (Ontario, Canada: W.W. Norton, 1988), 328.

they become a public speaker. Susan was fundamentally quiet and shy with a wicked and dry sense of humor. But I could no more get her to tell jokes to an audience of people at a cocktail party than I could get her to shave her head bald. For her part, she could not get me to stop being assertive, which was my base nature. We strove to accept each other for who we were and didn't try to impose demands that the other change. It formed part of the core element of a successful relationship.

However, this is different from our earlier discussion about love being a catalyst for change in ourselves. That refers to the motivation to change from within to do something that improves yourself and pleases the other person. Very different. For Susan, that meant a concerted effort to overcome her shyness and not stay in a corner at business or related events that we attended together, which she would have preferred but would have reflected poorly on me. Instead she forced herself to mingle and strike up conversations with strangers. She called it "Being Mrs. Phil." And for myself, I had to become more attuned to the emotional aspects of what was going on around me and in relationships in particular. I had to disregard my usual rational approach to everything and habit of looking at every situation as an exercise in logical decision-making. Of course not everything in a relationship is rational. For instance, I had to appreciate the emotional aspect of Susan's relationship with her children rooted in their childhood, which was different than my relationship with my children. If I were to impose my rational expectations on her interactions with her children, I ran the risk of adversely affecting our relationship. So emotional attunement to her family was a change I made from within. Both of these are examples of change from within inspired by love, not attempts to change the other from without.

Fromm tells us that to love another person, we must feel at one with them, but with them "*as they are,*" not as we may need them to be as an object for our own use.[100] If both parties follow this advice and make the required commitment to the relationship, then Person

---

100   Erich Fromm, *The Art of Loving* (New York: Harper & Row, Inc., 1956), 26.

says the approach the couple takes toward each other in times of disagreement will be more open and accepting of the other. To survive as a couple, she says, issues must be resolved, not shoved under the rug. For love to thrive, the couple must compromise, settle the issues between them, and declare their unity and common purpose. Above all, the couple itself, or the "we," must have top priority.[101]

One of the first potential areas of disagreement between Susan and me was over her family's pets. She was an animal lover, and I was not. She had a small Shih Tzu/Yorkie, Sammy—originally her daughter's dog—that had become her responsibility before we met when her daughter changed colleges. I couldn't complain; he was a cute little thing and not a big presence in her apartment. After we moved in together, however, her son had the same problem with his large shepherd-mutt mix, Charlie, and Susan wanted to take him also. I initially balked, not wanting to have two dogs in the apartment. But I saw this had the potential to be a major bone of contention. She wanted the dog that her son couldn't keep, and no other options existed. Putting him down wasn't an option I could advocate, for many reasons. The "we" of the family was no longer limited to the two of us. We now had Sammy and Charlie too. After discussion, she agreed to assume full responsibility for walking, grooming, and feeding them if I would embrace the "new family" without complaint. Our deal allowed us to continue united, albeit in a more crowded household.

As it turned out, Charlie took to me more than Susan. When I worked at my desk, he'd lie at my feet while I worked, and he slept on the floor on my side of the bed. Somehow, he wormed his way into my heart despite my palpable reservations. That meant of course that our compromise went out the window because I took care of Charlie as much as Susan did. Funny how difficulties have a way of working themselves out if the parties approach them sensibly and up front.

Throughout this process, however, there is one more rule

---

101   Ethel Spector Person, *Dreams of Love and Fateful Encounters: The Power of Romantic Passion* (Ontario, Canada: W.W. Norton, 1988), 66.

that must be followed. Experts agree that neither individual in a relationship should relinquish their individuality or identity. As the Pawelskis point out, healthy relationships are characterized by interdependence, in which our partner doesn't "complete" us but rather "complements" us. Each person is secure, mature, and whole, while also being vulnerable and open to the other. Echoing Aristotle, this kind of relationship is one in which each person appreciates the unique strengths of the other and benefits from the mutual giving and receiving of support.

For Person, this state of being arises when the lovers establish an optimal distance between them that allows for union without the use of domination or submission that subverts autonomy. There must be what she calls a "mutual accommodation" to both intimacy and separation. She observes that "individuals best able to maintain the paradoxical stance required in love—the ability to achieve union without compromising autonomy and to tolerate aloneness without collapse of the self—are often those with a strong sense of self . . ."[102]

Maryanne Fisher, too, warns that one of the roadblocks to a genuine loving relationship is the failure to maintain a sense of self and an individual identity as we create an "interdependent" relationship.[103]

According to Fromm, the only kind of person who can successfully enter into and maintain such a strong relationship is one who has achieved a certain degree of maturity and character development. He believes this is someone who has attained "a predominantly productive orientation; in this orientation the person has overcome dependency, narcissistic omnipotence, the wish to exploit others or to hoard, and has acquired faith in his own human powers, [and] courage to rely on his powers in the attainment of his goals."[104]

I know that this is one of the reasons Susan and I succeeded as a couple. We were both mature and already had strong, well-

---

102   Ibid., 328.
103   Maryanne Fisher and Victoria Costello, *The Complete Idiot's Guide to the Chemistry of Love* (New York: Penguin Group, 2010), 53.
104   Erich Fromm, *The Art of Loving* (New York: Harper & Row, Inc., 1956), 24.

formed identities that neither of us was willing to subjugate. I often felt that Susan's quiet confidence, charm, and grace complemented my sometimes bull-in-a-china-shop approach to life.

Knowing ourselves in this mature way isn't enough on its own, however. We must know the other person equally as well. Thomas Lewis and his colleagues describe loving as "synchronous attunement and modulation." Adult love, they assert, is dependent upon knowing the other. They describe true love as deriving from intimacy—"the prolonged and detailed surveillance of a foreign soul."[105]

Fromm agrees, saying that "to respect a person is not possible without knowing him." He says that care and responsibility would be blind "if they were not guided by knowledge, and knowledge would be empty if it were not motivated by concern." But respect is only possible when we've achieved the independence that allows us to "walk without needing crutches" and without having to dominate or exploit another. As Fromm says, "Respect exists only on the basis of freedom: 'L'amour est l'enfant de liberté,' as an old French song says; love is the child of freedom, never that of domination."[106]

A relationship built on mutual respect occurs when the individuals complement each other and where each partner maintains a sense of self and individual identity in a union. It occurs when the relationship is an expression of romantic collaboration, and not domination, where each treats the other person as their best self would want to be treated, when each partner loves the other as is, not for what they think they can get from them. A perfect example from the annals of history is the marriage of Pierre and Marie Curie.

Pierre Curie was an established physicist and chemist in the 1890s in Paris where he headed a famous laboratory. In 1884, Marie, after obtaining degrees in mathematics and physics at the Sorbonne, started working with him in his laboratory. They fell deeply in love

---

105   Thomas Lewis, Fari Amini, and Richard Lannon, *A General Theory of Love* (New York: Random House, 2000), 207.
106   Erich Fromm, *The Art of Loving* (New York: Harper & Row, Inc., 1956), 27.

and married within a year; they had two children and worked together in his lab, both side by side and on their own individual projects. A colleague had discovered radiation years earlier, but an electrometer that Pierre built for Marie for her research exposed a separate mineral that contained radiation. In 1898, through collaboration, they discovered two radiating elements they called polonium (after her native country Poland) and radium. They continued to work together and in 1902 discovered and coined the term *radioactivity* to explain how the decay of atomic nuclei causes radiation. The next year, 1903, Pierre got nominated for the Nobel Prize in Physics but complained that his wife deserved the award equally. That year they were both awarded the Nobel Prize for their radiation research, making Marie the first female Nobel laureate.

Everyone who knew them noted that they were devoted to each other until Pierre's untimely death in 1906 in an accident on a Paris street. Marie dedicated herself to continuing the research they had begun, and the Sorbonne offered her the post that Pierre had held as lecturer and head of the lab. She became the first female lecturer at the Sorbonne and was appointed professor. In 1908, she received a second Nobel Prize in Chemistry for her work in isolating pure radium.

Not everyone can hope to achieve what the Curies' deep love for each other achieved. But they are a famous example of how partners can achieve more together in love than individually. They are an example we can use to strive for in our relationships.

PUTTING THE RULES INTO ACTION

Interestingly, the Pawelskis, a loving couple who also work together, suggest that a satisfying relationship requires "active virtue," not just a theoretical knowledge of what we should do. And it goes without saying that this virtue must be practiced over and over again throughout your lifetime together, not just once or twice or even intermittently. It's also a necessity to adhere to Fromm's advice to be in a "constant state of active concern with the loved one."

When we turn thoughts into action, our actions may, over time, become habits. The Pawelskis cite American philosopher William James, who contended that there are great benefits to developing habits. The first is increased competence, and the second is decreased effort. Once you learn how to tie your shoes, you no longer need to think about it. Putting thoughts into action so that they become habitual will not only benefit you but also your partner and will continually strengthen your relationship. We had a habit of a giving each other a gentle kiss on the lips before we turned the lights out for sleep each night. We joked, halfheartedly, that if either of us didn't wake up in the morning, at least we'd have kissed the other goodbye. I also got into the early habit of calling her dear, not Susan, which for me was much more intimate than her given name, which everyone else called her. No one else called her dear!

There's an additional framework that will support your actions in building a lasting relationship. The field of *positive psychology* focuses on human strengths and potential, and it celebrates what is best in life, such as well-being, satisfaction, happiness, interpersonal skills, perseverance, talent, wisdom, and personal responsibility. Positive psychologists study the impact of passion, gratitude, savoring, and spirituality on our well-being in order to understand what qualities and feelings make life fulfilling and worth living. Many people believe that their happiness is a result of what happens to them, while positive psychologists assert that happiness is largely a result of how we choose to *respond* to what happens to us. By learning how to respond more positively to the events in our lives, we can strongly influence the quality of our experiences.[107]

Again, this approach is based on Aristotle's teachings and also on the idea that our happiness needs to be under our own control. To me, this sounds much like Buddhism, which also teaches that happiness is an internal construct that comes from how we respond to external

---

107   Suzann Pawelski and James O. Pawelski, *Happy Together: Using the Science of Positive Psychology to Build Love That Lasts* (New York: Penguin Random House (2018), 17.

events. When we're grateful for what we have rather than troubled by what we don't have and when we see the positive rather than the negative, we reduce our suffering and increase our happiness.

To illustrate the benefits of positive psychology on a relationship, the Pawelskis discuss the helpfulness of positive emotions and states, such as gratitude, serenity, interest, hope, pride, amusement, inspiration, awe, and love, which they consider to be an emotion. They cite scientific research that shows how these emotions have been helpful in making study participants more creative and better able to solve complex problems.[108]

They also cite research by Barbara Fredrickson, professor of psychology and director of the Positive Emotions and Psychophysiology Laboratory at the University of North Carolina. Fredrickson reports that people who experience more positive emotions possess lower levels of stress-related hormones and higher levels of beneficial hormones, which have positive physical and psychological effects. She has found that these types of people become "more optimistic, more resilient, more open, more accepting and more driven by purpose."[109] As a result, these people have stronger and more satisfying social relationships, and the good times they share are buffers against the tough times. In the case of marital relationships, the good times protect against divorce.[110]

It isn't hard to see how positive psychology can benefit romantic relationships. In fact, according to the Pawelskis, Fredrickson found through laboratory experiments that positive emotions can help people feel closer and more connected to their loved ones.[111] Positive emotions can benefit relationships through what the Pawelskis call "emotional contagion," which happens on an unconscious level when we pass along our feelings to our partner.[112]

Human beings tend to copy or synchronize with the facial

---

108   Ibid., 75.
109   Ibid., 91.
110   Ibid., 76.
111   Ibid., 79.
112   Ibid.

expressions, vocalizations, postures, and behaviors of those around us. As we learned in chapter 5 when discussing Thomas Lewis and his coauthors' concept of limbic resonance, we can actually "catch" the emotions of our partner, whether negative or positive. This phenomenon can have either positive or negative consequences depending on whether the emotions conveyed are positive or negative. Negative emotions can cause us to become angry, anxious, or withdrawn. Negativity can impede our ability to find solutions to problems, and it can even spiral downward to hopelessness until we no longer feel it's worth making an effort in the relationship.

On the other hand, positive emotions can foster love. In Barbara Fredrickson's book *Love 2.0*, she expands upon limbic resonance with her own concept of "positivity resonance," which she describes as a tightly woven, threefold event: (1) a sharing of one or more positive emotions between you and your partner; (2) a synchrony between you and your partner's biochemistry and behaviors (the Pawelskis' emotional contagion or Lewis et al.'s limbic resonance); and (3) a reflected motive to invest in each other's well-being that bestows mutual care.[113]

This third aspect is nearly identical to Fromm's "constant state of alertness and awareness" and is triggered by positive emotions. Fredrickson asserts that "any moments of positivity resonance that ripple through the brains and bodies of you and another can be health and life-giving."[114] She concludes that couples that regularly carve out time to do novel and exciting things together enjoy higher-quality marriages. She offers some very simple examples such as dancing, hiking, or attending a musical performance or play. The Pawelskis, too, suggest cooking dinner together from scratch, watching a movie, or going for a long walk in nature.

We can find further scientific support for engaging in these types of activities from Dr. Helen Fisher, who recounts how her Chinese

---

113   Barbara L. Fredrickson, *Love 2.0, How Our Supreme Emotion Affects Everything We Feel, Think, Do and Become* (New York: Penguin Group, 2013), 17.
114   Ibid., 35.

colleague, Mona Xu, conducted fMRI mapping of seventeen young Chinese couples that were passionately in love. The researchers discovered that the same areas of their brains lit up as those of their American counterparts. Four years later, the researchers revisited the same couples and found that eight of them were still together. When they compared the brain scans of those eight pairs with the scans of those who had split up, they discovered that those who were still in love showed specific brain activity associated with the ability to suspend negative judgment and engage in overevaluation of their partner—what psychologists call "positive illusion." The couples focused on the positives in their partners rather than the negatives. Such scientific evidence bolsters the argument that practicing positive emotions has a neurological basis in helping to promote healthy, loving relationships.

This concept is expressed well in the poem "The Meaning of Love" by Krina Shah:

To love is to share life together,
to build special plans just for two,
to work side by side,
and then smile with pride,
as one by one, dreams all come true.

To love is to help and encourage
with smiles and sincere words of praise,
to take time to share,
to listen and care
in tender, affectionate ways.
To love is to have someone special,
one on whom you can always depend
to be there through the years,
sharing laughter and tears,
as a partner, a lover, a friend.

To love is to make special memories
of moments you love to recall,
of all the good things
that sharing life brings.
Love is the greatest of all.

I've learned the full meaning
of sharing and caring
and having my dreams all come true
I've learned the full meaning
of being in love
by being and loving with you.

(© Krina Shah, Published August 2008)

In the next chapter, I'll tell you more about how Susan and I put these concepts into daily practice, even though we weren't consciously aware of it at the time. In retrospect, it's surprising to me that we did so much without consulting any source about what would help strengthen our bond.

CHAPTER 8

My Relationship with Susan: How We Followed the Experts' Advice Without Knowing It

I need love, love
To ease my mind,
And I need to find time
Someone to call mine.

My mama said,
"You can't hurry love,
No, you'll just have to wait,"
She said, "Love don't come easy,
It's a game of give and take."
You can't hurry love,
No, you just have to wait,
You gotta trust; give it time,
No matter how long it takes.

("You Can't Hurry Love" by Brian and Eddie Holland Jr.
and Lamont Dozier; popularized by The Supremes)

S usan and I were a perfect example of how you can't hurry love. As I mentioned earlier, we brought a bit of maturity into our venture. When we met, I was fifty-nine, and she was fifty-four. Right from the beginning, we had the utmost respect for each other's intelligence and competence. Neither of us entered into the relationship thinking we were better or smarter than the other. This mutual respect permeates my **Don'ts** and **Dos**, which you'll read later. These are a distillation of the rules found throughout the book.

Like any couple, we had occasional disagreements, of course, but we always talked them through calmly and respectfully. We supported each other from day one. Susan was an architect, working for a company that she believed wasn't treating her commensurate with her contributions to the business. She didn't see a future for herself there, so I suggested she strike out on her own and form a consulting company. She hadn't even considered that option at the time, but I told her how impressive and competent she sounded on the phone when discussing her work. I reminded her that she had previously started and run a successful business. She had designed pieces of furniture, had them built in Guadalajara, Mexico, and then sold them for a comfortable profit to Americans who owned property in Playa del Carmen. I convinced her that if she had accomplished that, there was no reason she couldn't succeed independently doing what she was trained to do as an architect.

After researching the possibilities and speaking to people about how to find business, she launched her firm and landed an account with a company that made floor-to-ceiling sliding glass doors. She began as their New York metropolitan representative and then took over the East Coast, eventually becoming their national salesperson. She was thrilled that she had taken the leap to work for herself.

I didn't know it at the time, but I had done what the experts propose we all do, which is support our partner in any way we can. There was no conscious thought on my part that encouraging her would strengthen our bond. It simply felt like the right thing to do for the woman I cared about. The side effect was that it brought us closer together because she clearly saw my faith in her, and when she started to succeed, she felt good about herself.

At that time, I hadn't yet read Aristotle or the Pawelskis' book, both of which advocate consciously looking for positive traits in the other person as a vehicle for securing the relationship. It happened organically between us.

Of course, the support was mutual. As a trial lawyer, I prepared heavily to get cases ready in the weeks leading to trials. It was a dramatically new lifestyle for Susan, but she never questioned the time I had to spend or my singled-minded focus on trial preparation and the trials themselves. When we first started living together and throughout our entire relationship, she gave me as much time as I needed without complaint. In fact, she accommodated my trial schedule by making dinner at the end of my preparation for the day, typically around 8:00 or 9:00 PM, which was at least two hours later than her preferred mealtime. Out of respect for my needs, she supported me and put my interests before her own—something that didn't go unnoticed by me.

YOUR CHILDREN

Another indication of the respect we had for each other was that neither of us ever tried to interfere or influence the other's relationship with their children, unless one of us asked the other for advice. Our children were grown and didn't live with us, so we didn't have to contend with how to raise them.

Occasionally, I overheard conversations she had with her children, and I thought about how I might have responded or behaved differently. I've no doubt Susan had similar feelings when she heard my conversations with my children. But we both knew instinctively that it would be counterproductive and possibly even create resentment if one of us tried to tell the other how to handle their children.

I have heard stories of parents who defer to a new partner in the disciplining of their children, and there are other cases in which people want their new partner to take an active role in disciplining children who live at home. While such a complex topic is beyond the scope of this book, the rules I offer here, along with my *Don'ts* and *Dos* list, can be applied to any relationship where there are children because they are based not only on my relationship with Susan but on advice from a wide array of experts. Obviously, when you have children living with you, there will be greater demands on your time and increased challenges. But unless you want to be two ships passing in the night, it's crucial that you make time to do the things suggested to have a relationship that survives after the children leave home. There is no one set of rules for couples without children and another for couples with children.

Regardless of the understanding you have about how you deal with your respective children, the respect you give your partner must apply to their children as well. No matter what you think, it won't advance your relationship to criticize your partner's parenting skills or to find fault with their children.

As I recounted in chapter 4, I decided in our third year together that I wanted to call Susan my "wife" rather than my "significant other" because as my son Tom joked when he roasted me at our wedding, "Everyone knows Dad is the marrying kind!" But before I proposed, I asked both of her children if it was okay that I ask their mom to marry me. This gesture of respect for them solidified my role as the head of the family and helped me gain their love and respect from then on.

As for the marriage proposal itself, I asked Susan to meet me at the restaurant bar where we had first met. I arrived early and chose the exact seats we'd had two years earlier, putting the engagement ring, prominently displayed in its robin's-egg-blue box, on the bar in front of the seat next to me, so that she'd see it as soon as she sat down. When she did, she screamed with joy and immediately called her daughter Lindsay, who responded, "Mom, I already knew what Phil was going to do." I imagine knowing ahead of time pleased

Lindsay enormously and put me in her good graces. As an added bonus, Susan was thrilled that I had included her children in such a significant life event. Five years later when Lindsay got married, she returned the favor. Naturally, her father gave a toast at her reception, but Lindsay asked me to do so as well, which was a wonderful surprise. It meant the world to me that she felt so comfortable asking me to speak in front of her family and friends, and it showed how successfully Susan and I had brought our families together.

Susan showed her love and respect for my children as well. For example, when my first grandchild, Leonardo, was born, she immediately set up a bank account for him with a generous first deposit earmarked for education. She never mentioned it to me, and I didn't hear about it until my son Matthew told me he received the bank statement. This kind and generous act forever endeared Susan to my children.

THE IMPORTANCE OF ACTIVITIES TOGETHER

Engaging in activities together puts your love "into action," which brings you closer together and is supported by positive emotional communication. All of this strengthens your relationship. This behavior, whether intuitive or conscious, fosters positive emotions that flow back and forth in an "emotional contagion" or "limbic resonance dance" between the two of you.

Susan and I both enjoyed going out to movie theaters, as well as streaming movies at home. We would set aside one night a week to see a movie and go to dinner afterward, or we would stay home and binge-watch Netflix's *House of Cards*, rooting against Francis Underwood, while one of us prepared a simple meal and the other cleaned up. We didn't do this with any long-term goal in mind for our relationship, but it still strengthened our bond.

Another example of an activity that strengthened our relationship was exercising (no pun intended!). I regularly exercised at a gym, and Susan usually attended exercise classes or went on bike rides. I encouraged her to try weight training, which was new to her, taking her to my gym and teaching her how to use the weight machines. At first, we worked out together, but eventually, she began doing it on her own while I continued with my own routines. Even so, we continued to interact and joke around during our workouts.

Susan cared a great deal about her appearance, so when she began to notice muscle definition that looked good, she was pleased with the work she had done and encouraged by the results. I introduced her to a trainer, and she enjoyed working out with him. After she died, he told me that when they first started working together, she handed him a picture of Sharon Stone with the order, "Otto, this is what I want to look like!" He still has the picture in his locker.

The experts advise engaging in new activities together to create shared interests and further strengthen the bonds of love. I suggested weight training because I thought it would be a healthy thing for Susan to do. I had no idea that we were participating in an activity that would help solidify our emotional ties to one another.

Yet another activity that brought us closer together was gardening, a hobby that Susan and I both loved. As I mentioned in chapter 4, we purchased a modest second home on the east end of Long Island in a town we both liked. It gave us the opportunity to participate in a "garden renovation" of the entire front and back yards. We were both experienced with gardening, so it was more like two army platoons joining forces to initiate a campaign.

We planned the renovation together, and other than the removal of some trees and large bushes, we did all the work ourselves. The rose garden was Susan's particular area of expertise, while I did the heavy-lifting phase of replenishing the sandy soil with new dirt, compost, peat moss, and fertilizer. But then we both went to work planting and tending to our joint pet project. We didn't realize that we were growing our relationship along with the flowers, but it provided yet another vehicle for praising each other and building trust and confidence in one another.

I teased Susan that she probably thought the comment in my Craigslist ad about how I "enjoy gardening" was merely a "come on." But then I looked around and said, "Now look where we are!" She smiled and nodded in agreement. Below is a photo that I took of her as we worked together in our garden during the first summer that we owned the house. It turns out that we were also creating and reinforcing our own *new history* together—"our story"—which we then shared with others. Creating your "story" is another suggestion from experts for building and reinforcing a relationship.

One of our new activities occurred when Susan bought me dance lessons as a birthday gift. I have always enjoyed dancing, and Susan had taken tap lessons when she moved to New York City after her divorce. As a result, we both improved our abilities and were always eager to step onto the dance floor at weddings and parties.

As a caution, however, the Pawelskis cite Robert Vallerand, professor of social psychology at the University of Quebec, Montreal, and past president of the International Positive Psychological Association, who explains that the idea behind doing things together is to have fun rather than to compete with each other. If you take up tennis, for example, don't get into heated and competitive matches to determine who is the better player. If you go swimming, don't race. It may not be a good idea to engage in activities in which one of you is superior if there's too good a chance the other will lose interest.

Susan and I discovered this when we tried to golf together. Her mother was an excellent golfer, and she encouraged Susan to play when she was a teenager. But Susan didn't continue with it. As a result, when we tried to play together, she was self-conscious and didn't want to play with anyone else. This is difficult since golfers generally play in foursomes, but I managed to convince her otherwise.

Golf etiquette requires that you move along so you don't hold up the people behind you. Susan took a long time over the ball on every shot and took her sweet time walking from one shot to the next, which delayed everyone else. I continually asked her to move on, which she resented. We quickly realized golf wasn't a pleasurable experience for either of us. Instead, we agreed that I would play golf while she made pottery. That way neither of us felt abandoned by the other in favor of their hobby.

We maintained our separate interests and friends throughout our marriage, which was beneficial to our relationship. She had her friends, and I had mine. We knew instinctively and from past experience that it's important to maintain a degree of independence from one another. This was equally true when it came to our relationships with friends. Though we introduced one another to our respective friends and spent time with them as a couple, neither of us insisted that we only see our friends together.

She never complained when I went on a long weekend golf trip, and I didn't mind when she visited out-of-town friends or family. We spent plenty of time together but gave each other space, which made coming together again all the more satisfying, whether the time apart was a few hours or a few days. This behavior is closely aligned with the independence we discussed in chapter 7 as recommended by all the experts.

We tried new things in the bedroom as well. As is true with most new love, in the beginning, we couldn't keep our hands off of each other and made love whenever we could. That lustful desire naturally waned over time, but we were always open to experimenting and making love in new places, something that kept our interest alive throughout our time together (until she got cancer, of course, when sex was the last thing on our minds).

COMMUNICATION

We also discussed in the last chapter that all experts advocate finding methods to improve communication throughout your relationship. Susan and I, as it happened, were both list-makers to keep ourselves organized, and continuing this habit helped us to better communicate. We frequently laughed about this because we even had lists of our lists! Because of my work commitments and Susan's business schedule, as well as our many other activities, our daily organizational meetings were an essential tool of communication in our relationship. We would review our lists, plans for the day, what time I would be home, or if either of us had an engagement that would leave the other on their own for dinner that evening. We also asked if there was anything either one of us could do for the other that day.

This doesn't mean that our lists were always "rosy." Susan didn't suffer fools easily, so one of *her* lists was her "shit list." If you were unfortunate enough to get on it, you didn't come off. For example, one day the gardener's crew at our country house had pulled up what they thought were weeds but which were flowers that Susan had lovingly grown from seeds she smuggled from France. She was irate and blamed the gardener for not supervising his crew. No matter what this poor guy did to appease her after that incident, he couldn't get off her list.

So our lists covered both the good and the not so good, but our morning briefings were primarily organizational. We saved the not so good for more appropriate times. These briefings kept the channels of communication open and demonstrated our thoughtfulness toward each other—two of the most important elements of a healthy relationship.

Occasionally, these conversations would reveal a difference of opinion about an event or something with regard to our respective children. But we knew that this brief morning meeting wasn't the right time to expand on those issues, since we were both about to start our day. So whenever an issue needed resolution, we usually set a time later that same night or the next night when we could discuss it in greater detail. The extra time to thoughtfully consider our words before returning to the discussion proved an extremely beneficial strategy. We intuitively created a system that enabled us to keep lines of communication open while reinforcing our care for one another and strengthening our relationship.

Finally, Susan and I did something else all experts advise—we talked about what we were experiencing and how we felt about it. This began when we started dating, especially after we first slept together. We didn't understand it in terms of the psychological benefits, but we were mindful about the growth of our relationship and savored it.

For example, in July of 2007, after we had been together for only a month, I sent Susan the following email:

> Thank you for your thoughts. They are appreciated. But I think we are not only responding to each other's passion in the bedroom. I think we are recognizing values and attributes in each other that we see expressed in our respective work and family life that makes us respect each other and attracts us to the other. I also think we realize, consciously or not (see today's *NY Times* Science section about the subconscious mind), that such a process, assuming it continues the way it has been going, creates the foundation for a truly intimate and lasting relationship.

And I think we both recognize the value and benefit of such a relationship. So I think that these factors are fueling the passion in the bedroom because they generate the desire to please each other, which then feeds each other's passions, and we end up satisfied that we have pleased the other person and have been sated ourselves in the process. The sex and attraction to each other can't be this good without an emotional component driving it, which I believe comes from what we see and like about each other . . . outside of the bedroom. Maybe this is all self-evident to you, but I felt compelled to express it.

I only found this email recently while I was writing this book. It was in a folder in the back of her drawer in the desk that we shared. I have no idea why I was drawn to that folder so long after Susan's death; it had been there for twelve years without my knowledge. But I was astounded to read what I had written so long ago. Unbeknownst to me, Susan had saved many of the emails we exchanged, and it's uncanny that just as we were beginning our relationship, I was writing about the very topics we're discussing in this book.

These prescient thoughts about the path we were embarking upon and what we hoped to achieve are startling to me today, especially because I had forgotten about my email and hadn't read any relationship books before I wrote it. Yet, it touches on virtually every important relationship issue I've come to learn.

To add to my surprise, Susan used several techniques in her response that also tend to develop strong relationships. These were different from the ones in mine, such as complimenting me and expressing specifically what she liked about me that was important to her:

You write such beautiful things. Perhaps neither of us was appropriately appreciated before. Maybe we both had a lot of love and passion to give, but when we let a little of it out, that love and passion was not appreciated and was therefore squandered. Now, as we let bits of it out, and it's appreciated and relished, we feel safer to behave that way and do things we wanted to do before. To me, it feels great to behave like this, and doing it lets me be the person I want and should be. I love listening to you—you are so smart. I have noticed that when you discuss something, you analyze the situation and sum it up so succinctly and offer interesting insights. You also don't boast or brag. Phil, I see the love and caring you are capable of when you are with your children, and their love and respect for you is just as obvious. I think we are both reacting to each other's passion in bed, but I'm not questioning that . . .

How did she know that twelve years later, I would be writing about how love in a good relationship can make you feel like the best person you could and want to be? It's remarkable to me that she expressed these thoughts and feelings after only one month into our relationship. There were no relationship books on her shelf either.

I believe this demonstrates what I have said about my relationship with Susan: we were lucky that most of the tactics experts advise came naturally to us. These notes we wrote to each other years ago were prophetic and seem to foreshadow the writing of this book.

THE FIVE-TO-ONE RATIO

I have given you some general rules for developing a long-lasting relationship, so now, let's outline specific things the experts advise to enhance and maintain the love you've found.

The best place to begin is with concrete suggestions from John Gottman, who reinforces the notion that positivity is critical to sustaining a healthy relationship. In his book, *Why Marriages*

Succeed or Fail, based on years of research examining the nature of interactions between happy and unhappy couples, he maintains that for a marriage (or relationship) to succeed, there must be a *five-to-one* ratio of positive interactions (moments or feelings) between the partners to negative ones.[115] If negative events predominate or are equal, they destroy the fabric of the relationship and can lead to an inability to resolve conflicts. He offers examples of how to achieve the five-to-one ratio:

1. Show interest in what your partner is saying by acknowledging them rather than just "yessing" them.

2. Be affectionate outside of sexual intercourse, which Gottman refers to as "romantic contact." Hold your partner's hand, kiss them, and put your arm around them. Physical contact of any kind can bring you closer together. You can also express your love with words by reminding your partner of a happy time you experienced together.

3. Show you care with acts of thoughtfulness. Surprise them with flowers, buy tickets to the movie or concert they've talked about, cook their favorite meal, or simply call or text during the day to say "hello" and ask how they're doing. Stevie Wonder said it best with his love song "I Just Called to Say I Love You." His lyrics include phrases like "no New Year's Day," "in fact, here's just another ordinary day," and "I mean it from the bottom of my heart." The song is a perfect example of what Gottman recommends, and it can transform an average day into a memorable one.

4. Be appreciative by thinking about and verbally recognizing good things about your partner. Let them know you

---

115   John Gottman, *Why Marriages Succeed or Fail, and How You Can Make Yours Last* (New York: Simon & Schuster, 1994), 59–62.

feel lucky to have found them. Gottman points out that agreeing with your partner's ideas or solution to a problem is also a form of appreciation. Expressing pride in your partner strengthens the bonds between you. Who doesn't like to hear good things about themselves?

5. Show your concern for your partner when, for example, they express something distressing or troublesome to them, such as the illness of a friend or a problem at work. Acknowledge the importance of what they feel. Apologize if you did or said something that may have been thoughtless or insensitive, causing your partner hurt feelings or anger.

6. Be accepting even when you disagree with what your mate says. Listen and acknowledge that you understand their point of view but explain that you respectfully disagree. This reinforces the idea that you respect their views, even when you take an opposing position. Summarize what you heard them say *before* you respond to show that you've heard them and aren't disregarding their opinion. This technique also helps you to clarify any misunderstandings.

7. Show joy and excitement when the occasion presents itself. Gottman explains that while this may come naturally when things are going well, there will likely be times of stress when intentionally sharing good news could help return you both to more positive territory.

8. Be silly and witty with one another. Just fooling around together is a wonderfully positive experience. Sharing an "inside" joke, for example, is a way to nurture closeness.

THE BONDING POWER OF COOKING

As we learned in chapter 1, love is action. By thinking about your partner and how you can strengthen your connection using positivity, you can proactively create Gottman's five-to-one ratio of positive to negative interactions enjoyed by happy couples.

Cooking is one activity experts tell us has positive effects on the beginning and maintenance of an enduring relationship. *Evolution's Empress: Darwinian Perspectives on the Nature of Women*, which focuses on women's behaviors from an evolutionary perspective, discusses the influences of cooking. In the chapter "Women's Intrasexual Competition for Mates," Maryanne Fisher talks about how historically mothers and grandmothers have been the primary transmitters of food traditions. Cooking gave early humans an evolutionary advantage over other primates because it increased the quality of their diet, which led to larger brains and more leisure time.[116]

In other words, cooking may have been one of the first vitally important traditions in human history. It was during food preparation that rules regarding morals, the history of the people, proper social behavior, and even advice on marriage and sexual relations were transmitted from generation to generation.

In *The Oxford Handbook of Women and Competition*, Maryanne Fisher opens her coauthored chapter, "Food as a Means for Female Power Struggles," with a quote by Thomas Wolfe, world-renowned American novelist: "There is no spectacle on earth more appealing than that of a beautiful woman in the act of cooking dinner for someone she loves."[117] It's a powerful image, to be sure, and I can attest to its accuracy when I watched Susan cook. Clearly, food plays a significant role in the mating process even today.

---

116   Maryanne L. Fisher, Justin R. Garcia, and Rosemarie Sokol Chang, Editors, *Evolution's Empress, Darwinian Perspectives on the Nature of Women* (New York: Oxford Univ. Press, 2013), 123.

117   Maryanne L. Fisher, Editor, *The Oxford Handbook of Women and Competition* (New York: Oxford Univ. Press, 2017), 739.

Fisher and her coauthors discuss tactics used by women to outcompete same-sex rivals. They cite research (Walters and Crawford) that supports the idea that the two most frequently used methods to outcompete rivals are cooking (because it demonstrates domestic ability) and appearance. They also examine the traits that attract men to women and assert: "In the context of long-term commitment, men, on average, lower their premium on physical attraction and put greater emphasis on other desirable traits, such as loyalty and caring." Fisher and her coauthors also explain that cooking helps to highlight these traits in women, making them appear loving and caring toward others. They cite the 2013 *Oxford English Dictionary* definition of a "domestic goddess" as a "woman who excels at housework of all sorts but at cooking and baking in particular" to describe a woman who knows how to select and turn ingredients "into true feasts for her family and friends."[118]

They're quick to acknowledge, of course, that many women hate this female stereotype, saying that "those using feminist approaches would rather call these women 'domestic slaves' who comply to the wishes of others, in particular their children and partner." The authors stress that they aren't advocating for women to become domestic goddesses; they only seek to explain the evolutionary basis for why women all over the world still engage in cooking. They explain why (for some) cooking and baking capture the heart to such an extent that "it elevates women to the level of goddess" and how selecting and processing foods, as well as sharing food knowledge, can become genuine areas of female competition.[119] They also confirm that more research is needed to fully explore cooking as a female strategy to outcompete in same-sex competition.[120]

This competitive tactic of cooking doesn't just apply to females. The authors cite Walters and Crawford again, who reported that

118   Ibid., 740.
119   Ibid.
120   Ibid., 750.

"cooking lavish dishes" is one of the twenty-six strategies that *both men and women* use to outcompete same-sex competitors. In fact, that study found that there was no statistically significant difference between the sexes as to the frequency of engaging in the intrasexual competitive tactic of "attracting attention to domestic skill" by cooking a lavish meal and "demonstrating domestic skill" through time spent cleaning their home. Men and women both reported the same frequency of engaging in such competitive conduct.[121]

But for either sex to engage in this competitive behavior, knowing how to cook is important. As it turned out, and to my delight and good fortune, Susan was a fabulous cook and baker. Her idol was Martha Stewart. She had learned how to cook from Stewart's cooking shows and others and from the one hundred cookbooks she had amassed. She even took her daughter to meet Stewart at a cooking demonstration where she asked Martha to autograph her book for Lindsay.

Susan also showed her kindness to my children through her talent for cooking. I was used to eating out, but Susan insisted on cooking dinner three to four nights a week. I found this very appealing. Now that I've read about the evolutionary foundation of relationships, I recognize that she was using her cooking skills to transform a romantic relationship into a comfortable home together. Not only did she cook for me, but eventually, as occasions would arise, she cooked for my family. Her skills at using food to nurture warm feelings played a role during the very first summer weekend she spent at the beach house (staying in her own bedroom, of course).

On Saturday afternoon, I had played golf with a friend and planned a BBQ with my sons for that evening. Susan told me she was going to window-shop in town, but when I came home from golf, a spread of grilled vegetables, salads, cheeses, and dessert was waiting for us. She had taken it upon herself to do this for me and my sons, even though she hadn't met them. It was a wonderful surprise

---

121   Sally Walters and Charles B. Crawford, "The Importance of Mate Attraction for Intrasexual Competition in Men and Women," *Ethology and Sociobiology*, 15(1) (1994): 11, 14.

and had its intended effect of increasing my attraction to her and appreciation for her.

Cooking would play a significant role in our relationship as a way for her to express her love for me and my children and as an activity we engaged in together. For instance, the first winter we were together, we rented a ski house for a weekend. I don't ski, but Susan and her children did. So we invited her kids to join us, together with my sister and niece, considering the occasion an ideal opportunity to start introducing our families to each other. Susan and I cooked our first big meal together that weekend, taking turns with the prep work, cooking, and cleanup. Later that night, we looked at each other, smiling and nodding with satisfaction, and commented how we'd worked together effortlessly, as if we'd done it for years. It was a bonding experience.

We slowly introduced my three sons Tom, Matthew, and Peter, who were, respectively, twenty-nine, twenty-seven, and twenty-three at the time, to her son Danny, who was twenty-one, and her daughter Lindsay, who was nineteen. We discovered that gathering for meals that we cooked together was an ideal way to bring our children together. But make no mistake about it—Susan was the boss when it came to cooking, and I deferred to her. Most often, she'd organize and cook the meals while I did prep and cleanup. We reveled in our organizational skills and praised each other for what we each contributed, as well as the results we achieved in entertaining our children and encouraging them to become better acquainted.

Fisher and her colleagues note that women perceive cooking as joyful and a means to maintain the family identity, so they pass on cooking skills to their children. This behavior is referred to as "intergenerational caregiving." This is precisely what Susan did when she cooked for our families. She was the caregiver who fed the children, and she also taught her daughter how to cook. I witnessed this behavior firsthand, and I appreciated those traits of caring and nurturing. It reinforced to me that I had made the right decision to form a bond with her.

In the beginning of our courtship, the old saying "the way to a man's heart is through his stomach" was certainly true for me. Fisher and her coauthors discuss why this is so often the case and what was really going on in the early months of our relationship, most of which I wasn't aware of on a conscious level. As the authors explain, inviting someone into the private space of your home and sharing food together is an intimate act. When the *act* of cooking the food is added to the scenario, it becomes even more intimate than simply enjoying a meal together because cooking, caring, and commitment are so closely intertwined. The preparation and offering of food signal commitment to the receiver as well as the giver.

Fisher and her coauthors agree that people connect through many other means, but since cooking and caring have been so closely intertwined throughout our evolutionary history, it has come to be recognized as one of the most genuine signals of love and caring.

In an article entitled "Love and Food Have Always Been Intertwined," journalist Wency Leung cites Fisher's theory of the "inconvenience display."[122] This theory favorably compares the distance someone is willing to travel to see you as reflecting their level of interest with the extent of grocery shopping, menu planning, and slaving over a stove that creating a meal entails. Fisher calls this an "honest signal," since it's hard to fake and confirms the generally accepted view that feeding others is an expression of care. I certainly felt cared for when Susan cooked for me or for my children.

This and other research has revealed the scientific connection between food and love that many, especially those in ethnicities that consider food and family culturally intertwined, may have already suspected on a more unscientific level. Myrte Hamburg, Catrin Finkenauer, and Carlo Schuengel wrote about food offerings as "empathic emotion regulation."[123] This means that an offer of food is

---

122   Wency Leung, "Love and Food Have Always Been Intertwined," *The Globe and Mail Newspaper* (Toronto, ON, Canada: Feb. 2012).
123   Myrte E. Hamburg, Catrin Finkenauer, and Carlo Schuengel, "Food for love: the role of food offering in empathic emotion regulation," *Frontiers in Psychology*, 5:32 (2014).

motivated by and results in the regulation of the emotional state of both the provider and the receiver. They cite research that demonstrates eating behavior can strengthen relationships.[124] When two people were seen to offer each other food, observers rated their relationship as closer than when no food was offered. And when two people fed each other, their relationship was viewed as even closer. This research concluded that food sharing is an important nonverbal indicator of friendship and romantic involvement—more specifically, love.

Hamburg and her colleagues go on to cite research that showed meals are an important aspect of courtship behavior and that people ate together more often as their commitment increased.[125] They suggest that "closeness between the provider of the food and recipient should increase both due to the offer of food as a support behavior and due to the feelings of closeness and belongingness that the item of food may already represent for both provider and recipient."[126] Put simply, food offering as a support behavior can have a positive effect on interpersonal relationships.

This is all further scientific support for what I sensed at the time was the effect of Susan's cooking on us as a couple and on our families. It helped my sons get over their initial skepticism of this new woman in their dad's life and eventually endeared her to them. They saw that she was genuine and not simply trying to ingratiate herself with them. Food from Susan had a significant impact on my children's acceptance of her and on the successful integration of our families.

In her article, "Relationships: How to Connect with Others through Food," Chef Flavia Scalzitti points out that a meal shared together is a vehicle through which we create memories, and memories

---

124   Lisa Miller, Paul Rozin, and Alan P. Fiske, "Food sharing and feeding another person suggest intimacy: Two studies of American college students," *European Journal of Social Psychology*, 28(3),(1998): 423-436.
125   Myrte E. Hamburg, Catrin Finkenauer, and Carlo Schuengel, "Food for love: the role of food offering in empathic emotion regulation," *Frontiers in Psychology*, 5:32 (2014).)
126   Ibid., 38.

of events together are among the building blocks of relationships.[127] Our respective children still talk about meals we had together and recall funny stories that are now part of our new extended family's shared history.

Of course, as Maryanne Fisher reminds us, there's a close relationship between food, sex, and love. When we eat, we use many of the same senses used during sex, and feeding our lover enhances these sensations. So eating a meal together can, in a very real sense, be foreplay. A wonderful comedic example of this is the sensual and lascivious scene in the movie *Tom Jones*, which won the Oscar for Best Picture. Actors Albert Finney and Joyce Redman are elegantly dressed, with Joyce wearing a low-cut gown. As they eat with their hands, they stare at each other and play with the food in sexually suggestive ways. The scene builds to Redman slurping down an oyster given to her by Finney and rolling it around her mouth before finally swallowing it and leering at him with a come-hither grin. They immediately rush off arm in arm to the boudoir.

Another example that may come to mind for many is the scene in *9½ Weeks* in which Mickey Rourke blindfolds Kim Basinger and serves her from the refrigerator whatever he thinks might elicit a reaction, whether positive or negative.

THE IMPORTANCE OF "SAVORING"

We didn't know it at the time, but as it turned out, in preparing meals together, Susan and I enhanced and solidified our relationship by "savoring" what we had done. Savoring is a way to communicate your appreciation to your partner, which is something we did in our emails to each other, which I shared earlier. Savoring involves invoking mindfulness about an experience that goes beyond the

---

127   Flavia Scaizitti, "Relationships: How to Connect with Others Through Food" (http://momitforward.com/connecting-through-food, July 7, 2016)

initial experience itself.[128] The Pawelskis reference social psychologist Fred Bryant, the founder of the concept of savoring, who says that it may be the most effective way of communicating love to your partner. It isn't just a positive emotion but consciously attending to a good feeling that comes with a shared experience.

Reminiscing together about a past happy event is one example. By reliving a past positive event, you learn what makes you both thrive, and you're able to bring that past experience into the present.

When it's expected, however, note that gift giving is *not* savoring because it happens at the same time every year with birthdays, Valentine's Day, and other occasions. Savoring is most often spontaneous, mindful attention to your partner *in the moment*, which can be a powerful communication of love and care. A wonderful way to convey your love is through telling your partner how much you enjoy having them in your life, when it's unprompted and not connected to any special occasion. Obviously, if only one party in the relationship expresses this appreciation, they will feel neglected and unacknowledged. To be most effective in strengthening the relationship, these expressions should be reciprocal.

Below are the Pawelskis' five ways to savor, intended to increase the joy of a shared experience:

1. *Appreciative sharing and mutuality*: The best illustration of this is when partners jointly tell others the story of how they met, fell in love, and decided to move in together or get married. Sharing the details of your relationship is savoring it and conveys your commitment to one another. The inability to do this could signal that your relationship isn't as healthy as it should be. Susan and I regularly told people how we met on Craigslist because it was a

---

128   Susan Pawelski and James O. Pawelski, *Happy Together: Using the Science of Positive Psychology to Build Love That Lasts* (New York: Penguin Random House, 2018), 107.

surprising place to meet a future spouse. At the time, it was already turning into a site where you could also find a prostitute or unknowingly encounter an axe murderer. So we had the added bonus of some humor in our story.

2. *Self-disclosure*: Disclosing to your partner something about your past, whether positive or negative, opens up your world to them and can greatly strengthen your relationship by encouraging intimacy between you. Sharing something positive can elicit feelings of confidence or security from your partner, but negative experiences can create empathy or compassion, which also bring people closer. Susan and I were both open about our previous marriages and other relationships, and it helped create trust between us.

3. *Minding*: Pay careful attention and consciously attend to your partner's needs. This directive from the Pawelskis is virtually identical to Erich Fromm's concept of continual attentiveness, discussed in chapter 7. In addition to staying aware of each other's emotional needs, you can also celebrate and show appreciation for the good things your partner does. I frequently told others in Susan's presence about her success in business and the projects she was working on. Likewise, she often sang my praises about my success with cases in my practice. This behavior created warm feelings that flowed back and forth between us, confirming that we were both paying attention to the other's needs.

4. *Collaboration*: This involves undertaking a joint project without competitiveness or the need to impress or dominate. Working together to accomplish a task, such as planning a family vacation or just planning and cooking a

meal together, creates closeness. The biggest joint project I worked on with Susan was our second house, where we made virtually every renovation and decorating decision together. This took years and was a continual source of pride for us. We were thrilled to share our hard work with family and friends.[129]

As the Pawelskis describe, these projects can be "magical moments of connection" in which you enjoy and savor each other. My collaborations with Susan were some of the best times we had together and the strongest affirmations of our love for each other. Our joint effort on the house required multiple trips to stores to choose mundane items like faucets, lights, and doors. It might be surprising to hear that this huge undertaking happened early in our relationship. We met in 2007 and bought the house in 2008 before we got married in 2009. So, our collaboration on the house played a significant role in solidifying our relationship and validating our vision for our future together. In fact, I remarked to Susan when we closed on the house that even though we weren't married, buying property together was a real commitment. And the extensive work we did on it as a couple became a catalyst for further deepening our relationship.

The Pawelskis also point out that telling the story of your relationship and knowing when the other person is going to pause and when you're going to pick up where they left off is not only a collaborative effort but also a joint savoring of your experience.[130] So, it's two ways to savor one activity—double points!

---

129   Ibid., 117–118
130   Ibid., 118.

5. *Sexual empathy*: During lovemaking, it's important to be cognizant of your partner's feelings and respond to their needs. The Pawelskis tell us that people who feel emotionally affirmed in their relationships report greater enjoyment of sex. Suffice it to say, Susan and I had a very enjoyable sex life before she became sick.[131]

All of these suggestions have one thing in common—they value actively thinking about our partner in positive ways and use that positivity to enhance the relationship. Nothing suggested here is complicated; they simply require forethought and intentional attention to your mate. The seeds you sow with this behavior will almost always return a bountiful harvest of good feelings and love. If they don't, there may be an insurmountable impediment in your relationship that needs addressing. In other words, your efforts will either benefit your relationship or illuminate why the relationship may be in trouble. In either case, I hope you'll agree that the end result makes the discovery worth the effort.

The closeness you can achieve with your mate by following these behaviors is best expressed by e. e. cummings in one of his most famous and enduring poems, which captures the unity felt by two people who are deeply in love:

i carry your heart with me (i carry it in
my heart) i am never without it (anywhere
i go you go, my dear; and whatever is done
by only me is your doing, my darling)
i fear

no fate (for you are my fate, my sweet) i want
no world (for beautiful you are my world, my true)

---

131   Ibid.

and it's you are whatever a moon has always meant
and whatever a sun will always sing is you

here is the deepest secret nobody knows
(here is the root of the root and the bud of the bud
and the sky of the sky of a tree called life; which grows
higher than soul can hope or mind can hide)
and this is the wonder that's keeping the stars apart

i carry your heart (i carry it inmy heart)

CHAPTER 9

Ten Don'ts and Dos

This list is a condensed compilation of the experts' advice combined with what I learned from my relationship with Susan. It is an easy way for you to remember the most important points in this book so that you can apply them to your relationship on a day-to-day basis. Use them wisely!

DON'T

1. *Ever raise your voice to your partner when you have a disagreement.*

Susan and I were together for ten years, and while we didn't always agree on everything, neither of us ever raised our voice to the other. Not once. I recognize this may be difficult, some might even say impossible. But if you consider it objectively and rationally, you'll recognize that raising your voice or yelling at your partner immediately changes the dynamic of the conversation. If this behavior becomes habitual, it could negatively impact the relationship as a whole. The person on the receiving end is likely to become defensive, stop listening, and feel the need to defend or retreat, depending on the nature of the relationship and your individual personalities. None of these scenarios create good communication.

Psychologist and author Asa Don Brown writes in *Psychology Today*: "I have no reservations in saying that yelling decays the human spirit. It breaks the essence of the person receiving the vice, and it is unbecoming of the person enacting or engaging in the tantrum. . . . Yelling is a tantrum being propelled from one person and being received by another. Yelling is one of the most reprehensible acts of abuse."[132]

Raising your voice doesn't contribute in any positive way to resolving disputes and is instead likely to prevent reasonable dialogue. If you feel a need to raise your voice, walk away and calm down. Return when you feel able to continue the conversation in a positive way. If necessary, make an appointment to continue the discussion at a later time or on another day. This rule is invaluable to anyone who is serious about nurturing a good relationship because as in any other circumstance, merely saying something louder than the other person doesn't make you any more right.

It bears noting that in her current bestseller *Caste: The Origins of Our Discontent*, Isabel Wilkerson asserts that the real alpha dog does not have to raise their voice to command attention and obedience from the pack. "If you are having to raise your voice to get their attention, a dog will not see you as the leader. You have already lost. A true alpha does not behave like that and doesn't have to. If a so-called alpha resorts to that, they are signaling that they are not in control at all." She adds that calmness is the hallmark of a true leader. Bringing that attitude to any discussion in a relationship engenders trust and will enable harmonious communication instead of strife.[133]

One good way to avoid raising your voice and to maintain respect between the both of you is not to have any argument or serious discussion about a troubling issue when you are drinking. Alcohol

132   Asa Don Brown, "Please Yell, Me: The effects of yelling and verbal abuse," *Psychology Today* (Apr 21, 2017).
133   Isabel Wilkerson, *Caste: The Origins of Our Discontents* (New York: Random House, 2020), 208.

can impact your mood, behavior, thinking, and memory. Alcohol increases the amount of norepinephrine in the brain, which acts as a stimulant that can increase arousal and excitement, can also lower inhibitions, and increase impulsivity. That can make it difficult to consider the possible consequences of your actions or words you may use. The negative effect of this can be compounded because alcohol also decreases the activity of the prefrontal cortex, which is what helps you think rationally and clearly. Alcohol also slows down how information is processed in the brain, including interfering with understanding what you are feeling and thinking through potential consequences of your actions and words. This may result in your speaking without thinking, raising your voice and yelling, and saying things you would never otherwise say and may later regret. Situations can get out of hand rapidly and result in a shouting match rather than an intelligent discussion of whatever the problem is. If an issue arises between you and your partner and you have had a couple of drinks, it is best to agree to defer discussion until the next day when you are both in full control of your emotions, thoughts, and feelings so that you don't do or say something impulsively that may have negative consequences you would not have otherwise intended.

DON'T

2. *Ever call your partner a name (other than the pet name(s) you have for one another).*

Calling someone a derogatory name is an act of defiance and invites a negative response, whether verbally or internally. Sherri Gordon, an expert on bullying, says that "name-calling is one of the most damaging and painful types of bullying. It leaves victims with negative messages about who they are burned into their memories."[134] Bullying only adds

---

134   Sherri Gordon, "9 Consequences of Name-Calling," *verywellfamily.com* (Sept. 2019).

to the deterioration of any relationship. An example may be in order. For instance, don't tell your partner they are "acting like a bitch" it is the same thing as calling her a bitch. There can be nothing gained from using such a word except to put distance between you and her. And it is something so hurtful and derogatory she will never forget it and will take a lot to make up for. And your wife calling you "stupid" doesn't get anywhere in solving whatever the problem under discussion may be. Names like these force people to be more defensive and fight back, rather than opening up conversation. Once a name like this comes out of your mouth, it can't be taken back. You can't "unring" a bell. The damage is done. So stop yourself from ever calling your partner a name.

DON'T

3. *Criticize, condemn, or complain to your partner about something they do, especially in front of others.*

These three Cs are easy to remember. *Criticism* is a negative way to communicate displeasure. "You're lazy around the house" isn't going to motivate your partner. Expressing how the others' actions make you feel is a more productive way to air a grievance: "When you don't pick up after yourself, I feel like you don't care about the way our home looks. And it isn't fair to expect me to clean up after you, so if you could clean up after yourself, I'd really appreciate it." That's a more positive way of communicating without engaging in criticism.

To *condemn* is to pass judgment, but being judgmental isn't likely to solve the problem that you believe your partner's conduct has created. "Boy, are you wrong" is a judgment and is just as damaging as all the other ***Don'ts***.

We all have pet peeves about our partner's behaviors, but pick your battles and maintain perspective. No one likes to be on the receiving end of constant *complaining*, and it's almost never effective in changing behavior. If your partner regularly does something that irritates you, ask yourself if you're being hypersensitive or if they're *purposely* disrespecting your needs or wishes. If, after reflection, you believe you're justified, quietly and calmly explain why you feel that their behavior is disrespectful to you.

Finally, and most crucial to the health of your relationship, don't *ever* engage in these three Cs in front of others. Doing so only serves to embarrass your partner, stoke negative feelings, and add an unnecessary public dimension to your private argument. Humiliation isn't an effective communication technique.

DON'T

4. *Tell your partner what to do about their own issues, such as their children, their family, or their money, unless they specifically ask you for advice or guidance. If you find fault with something they do, discuss it in a civil manner.*

This rule particularly applies to second marriages and relationships in which one or both parties have children from a prior one. Offering your partner unsolicited advice about how they should raise their child is fraught with peril and can cause ongoing resentment, both from your partner and their children.

Remember that everyone parents differently. Don't take it upon yourself to discipline your partner's children unless you've discussed it and agreed that you will take on that important role. If they ask you to discipline their child, do it in a way that's consistent with how you discipline your own children. If your partner undermines your efforts and comes to the "rescue" of their child, making you the "bad guy," it will be a source of friction that could affect your relationship with their child. To avoid unnecessary strain, discuss parameters and agree on them early in the relationship.

The *Dos* are behaviors we've discussed at length throughout this book and on which almost all of the experts agree. The benefits of these behaviors are self-evident. Be proud to take the initiative to engage in them. They will make your partner happy and, as a result, will make you happy. What could be a more rewarding relationship than one in which both partners are happy?

DO

1. *Things for your partner without being asked, such as cooking, household chores, bringing home an unexpected gift, making a surprise reservation for dinner, or purchasing tickets to a play or concert.*

DO

2. *Talk to each other in person at least once a day and for at least thirty minutes without any distractions, perhaps at breakfast before your day begins or after dinner when you can be alone together.*

This means no phone, no internet, and no TV! If you have children, you may need to wait until after their bedtime.

This daily meeting is an opportunity to review your schedules for the upcoming day or to discuss what your day was like. It should be positive and constructive or at least neutral and not negative. If you have a grievance you'd like to air, schedule that talk for another time.

DO

3. *Always respect your partner.*

To quote Erich Fromm, "Respect is loving the person for who they are rather than who you need them to be for your own purposes." As he reminds us, respect is the ability to see a person as they are and to be aware of their unique individuality. It implies an absence of exploitation. He tells us that we should "want the loved person to grow and unfold for his own sake, and in his own ways, and not for the purpose of serving me."[135]

DO

4. *Participate in activities together like sports, dance, gardening, or volunteering.*

Entertain guests and share responsibilities of preparation, cooking, and cleaning. Travel, both to get away from the daily grind and to be alone together, whether on big trips or to local places. If possible, enjoy at least one night out per week as a couple, regardless of activity. Be supportive of the other in *their* hobbies.

The idea is to be collaborative. Plan and do it together without being competitive. Barbara Fredrickson says, "Couples who regularly carve out time to do novel and exciting things together, such as hiking, snowboarding, dancing, or attending musical performances and plays enjoy higher-quality marriages."[136]

DO

5. *Make an effort with your appearance and grooming habits to show that you care what your mate thinks of you.*

Dress nicely when you go out together to convey the message "this is important to you, so it's important to me." (Of course, if your partner doesn't have an opinion on grooming, feel free to skip over this bit of advice.)

---

135   Helen Fisher, *Anatomy of Love: A Natural History of Mating, Marriage, and Why We Stray* (New York: W.W. Norton & Company, Inc., 2016), 26.
136   Barbara L. Fredrickson, *Love 2.0, How Our Supreme Emotion Affects Everything We Feel, Think, Do and Become* (New York: Penguin Group, 2013), 35.

DO

6. *Give your partner the space they need to do their own thing—seeing friends and family without you, going to classes, having hobbies, etc. Doing everything together all the time will stifle one or both of you and can lead to resentment or claustrophobia.*

Obviously, it would be impossible to do *all* of these things *all* of the time. Three "briefings" a week, a kind remark on a regular basis, and a movie or intimate dinner (if possible) will go a long way to cementing your commitment to each other. If you do something that creates friction, anger, or disappointment, talk it over and begin again. Remind each other that today is the first day of the rest of your lives.

If you can follow these sometimes-challenging-but-always-rewarding rules *most* of the time, you can expect to enjoy a healthy, positive, lasting, and loving relationship with each other. Life will be worth living!

CHAPTER 10

Love and Death

Do not stand at my grave and weep
I am not there; I do not sleep.
I am a thousand winds that blow.
I am the diamond glints on snow.
I am the sunlight on ripened grain.
I am the gentle autumn rain.
When you awaken in the morning's hush
I am the swift uplifting rush
Of quiet birds in circled flight.
I am the soft stars that shine at night.
Do not stand at my grave and cry;
I am not there. I did not die.

("Do Not Stand at My Grave and Weep," by Mary Elizabeth Frye, 1932)

You might wonder why I felt the topic of death was an important one to include in a book on how to nurture and maintain a strong, loving relationship. A fair question. My purpose with this chapter is to show you that when you find and sustain a deep and lasting relationship, it will live on after death. We will see, both from my own personal experience and from the experiences of other writers, that strong relationships do not die but instead take on another form when one of the partners dies, however hard that may be to contemplate.

Bell hooks says that when we love deeply, our love is "stronger than death." She notes that love is the only force that allows us to hold another close beyond the grave. Love does not die with death, and in fact those who were deeply in love at the time of death experience a deepening of that love. She believes that those who have known that kind of love are more able to embrace its loss. When we know we have given our all, "when we have shared with them that mutual recognition and belonging in love which death can never change or take away," coping with its loss becomes easier.[137] If you have no regrets about what you contributed to the relationship and feel no incompleteness or sense that you could have done more, you are able to embrace death without feeling irredeemable regret. Under these circumstances, death becomes not an end to life but a part of the living.

Noted Dutch theologian and author Henri Nouwen espoused the belief that "those you have loved deeply and who have died live on in you, not just as memories but as real presences."[138] I believe this is true in a literal and physical sense. As we touched on when discussing limbic resonance in chapter 5, the memories we have are physically created by chemical and electrical encoding in the neurons in different areas of the brain. Depending on the type of memory, whether long, short, or working, these memories can usually be retrieved. The physical aspect of this means, to me, that in a very tangible way, the memory of the deceased is a physical component of our brain. Susan's memory is stored in my brain's memory vaults, so I will always carry her around with me. Thomas Lewis and his coauthors discuss this kind of loss in another way, by explaining that when someone loses a partner and expresses the feeling that a part of them is missing or gone, this is truer than even the survivor may realize. There is a palpable physical loss "because a portion of neural activity depends on the presence of that other living brain. Without it, the electrical interplay that makes up *him* has changed. Lovers hold keys to each other's identities and they

---

137   bell hooks, *All About Love* (New York: HarperCollins, 2000), 188.
138   Ibid., 189.

write neurostructural alterations into each other's networks. Their limbic tie influences who the other is and becomes."[139] Death short-circuits that connection.

The belief that love survives death and can grow after death is expressed, and in many ways validated, by writing about the deceased. The renowned poet Elizabeth Barrett Browning beautifully illustrated this concept in her famous "Sonnet 43," which describes her intense love for Robert Browning. It builds to a powerful and deeply moving last verse:

> *How do I love thee? Let me count the ways.*
> *I love thee to the depth and breadth and height*
> *My soul can reach, when feeling out of sight*
> *For the ends of being and ideal grace.*
> *I love thee to the level of every day's*
> *Most quiet need, by sun and candle-light.*
> *I love thee freely, as men strive for right.*
> *I love thee purely, as they turn from praise.*
> *I love thee with the passion put to use*
> *In my old griefs, and with my childhood's faith.*
> *I love thee with a love I seemed to lose*
> *With my lost saints. I love thee with the breath,*
> *Smiles, tears, of all my life; and, if God choose,*
> *I shall but love thee better after death.*

Scholars disagree about whether Elizabeth is referring to Robert's death, her own, or both of theirs after they are reunited, but bell hooks believes she is referring to Robert's death and how she feels about him after his death. However she meant it, it expresses the notion that love does not end when the body dies but survives death and can even grow in strength. Pulitzer Prize–winning American playwright and novelist

---

139   Thomas Lewis, Fari Amini, and Richard Lannon, *A General Theory of Love* (New York: Random House, 2000), 208.

Thornton Wilder recognized this effect of death on love. The last line of his classic *The Bridge of San Luis Rey* declares "there is a land of the living and a land of the dead and the bridge is love, the only survival, the only meaning."[140]

Author bell hooks believes that we honor the presence of our loved one "by naming the legacies they leave us. We need not contain grief when we use it as a means to intensify our love for the dead and dying, for those who remain alive." She references Browning's poem when she attests to the importance of memory and communion with our dead by those who remain loving them "better after death." By reenacting a habit of the loved one, talking or laughing about them, we invoke their memory. And though the grief may never leave us, we do not allow it to overwhelm us, and these expressions of memory become our way to pay homage to the deceased, to hold them close.[141]

Humorist, poet, and novelist Calvin Trillin wrote his book *About Alice* about his deceased wife, and it is a perfect example. Trillin never uses the word *love* to describe their relationship or how he felt about her, but the way in which he writes about her life, her accomplishments, her character, her foibles, and her strengths and weaknesses all pay homage to her and speak volumes about how deeply they loved each other. The last few lines of the book beautifully recount Alice's life, but also show us how difficult it was for him to cope with his grief. He explains that she had to have radiation treatment to fight cancer, but this treatment damaged her heart and, as a result, she died of cardiac failure. But the treatment had extended her life twenty-five years from her diagnosis and allowed her to watch her daughters grow up. "I know what Alice, the incorrigible and ridiculous optimist, would have said about a deal that allowed her to see her girls grow up: 'Twenty-five years! I'm so lucky.' I try to think of it in those terms, too. Some days I can and some days I can't."[142]

---

140   Thornton Wilder, *The Bridge of San Luis Rey* (New York: Harper Perennial Modern Classics, 2014).
141   bell hooks, *All About Love* (New York: HarperCollins, 2000), 203.
142   Calvin Trillin, *About Alice* (New York: Random House, 2006), 78.

I talk about Susan whenever an appropriate opportunity presents itself, either by telling a story about her that is relevant to the conversation or through sharing something she said or would have said about the situation at hand. She lives on when I share my memories of her with those around me.

As for finding love again after the death of a beloved, some may wonder if that is in any way a betrayal. But Ethel Person suggests that the readiness with which some widows and widowers fall in love after the death of a spouse speaks not to their callousness but to the magnitude of their loss. When a surviving spouse remarries, it can often be seen as a testament to the deceased, because it is an acknowledgment of longing for the connection that was felt so strongly with the deceased, a longing that comes from the loss of someone who was deeply loved.[143] The Jewish tradition, in fact, even teaches that the departed watches over their family, and if they see that their surviving partner is lonely and loveless, their soul becomes anguished. Their soul only finds true peace when the survivor finds happiness again. Thus, after an appropriate period of mourning, the survivor is expected to find love with another, both to assuage their own loneliness and for the benefit of the deceased's soul.

For my part, remarriage is not something I think about. I have no overwhelming desire to fall in love again. I can't imagine duplicating what Susan and I had.

For me, one of the greatest examples of love surviving death is found in the true story of the marriage of Mughal emperor Shah Jahan and Mumtaz Mahal in 1600s India. Mumtaz was the daughter of a Persian noble who had moved to India and held high office in the Mughal Empire. At fourteen Mumtaz became engaged to Shah Jahan, who was fifteen. They married five years later. As was the custom, he had other wives, but the official court chroniclers of the time reported that the others were marriages of convenience, for political reasons,

---

143   Ethel Spector Person, *Dreams of Love and Fateful Encounters: The Power of Romantic Passion* (Ontario, Canada: W.W. Norton, 1988).

and that he only loved Mumtaz. Shah Jahan's historian observed that "his whole delight was centered on this illustrious lady (Mumtaz) to such an extent that he did not feel towards the others (i.e. his other wives) one-thousandth part of the affection that he did for her."[144]

They were known to have had a beautiful, loving marriage. Mumtaz became his closest confidant and advisor regarding matters of state. For instance, she requested and got the Shah to commute death sentences and forgive enemies. She was the Shah's chief empress, to whom he gave the titles of Queen of the World, Queen of the Age, and Queen of Hindustan. Ultimately, he bestowed upon her the highest honor in the Muslim World, his Imperial Seal, the Mehr Uzaz.[145] Despite the fact that she accompanied him during battles, they managed to have fourteen children together.

They had been married nineteen years when she died during the birth of their fourteenth child. The Shah was inconsolable following her death and went into seclusion and mourning for a year.[146] It was reported that when he came back into public, his hair was white, he was stooped over, and his face was "worn."[147] To honor Mumtaz, he built a mausoleum for her repose through which he attempted to convey and memorialize his undying love and devotion to her throughout their life together. English poet Sir Edwin Arnold described it as follows: "Not a piece of architecture, as other buildings are but the proud passion of an emperor's love wrought in living stones." It is the Taj Mahal.

Many people have written poems, books, and stories in an effort to permanently explain the extent and depth of the love they feel for a spouse after their death. But the Taj Mahal, one of the most beautiful buildings ever erected in the world? That really says it all about love surviving death. This book is my Taj Mahal!

The final word for me about my love for Susan surviving her death comes from the famous song, "I'll Be Seeing You," which dates

---

144   Giles Tillotson, *Taj Mahal* (Wonders of the World) (Cambridge, MA: Harvard University Press, 2008), 30.
145   Mumtaz Mahal (https://en.wikipedia.org/wiki/Mumtaz_Mahal)
146   Ibid.
147   Ibid.

to 1938. We had a private family memorial for Susan, during which we spread her ashes in Three Mile Harbor, where she loved to drive our little boat. Pato Paez, whom I think of as another of my sons, and his husband, Brian Harris, were there with us, and Brian played guitar and sang this song. The words were originally intended for an entirely different purpose, but somehow Brian recognized they were appropriate for this occasion—and the rest of our lives.

I'll be seeing you
In all the old familiar places
That this heart of mine embraces

All day and through
In that small café
The park across the way
The children's carousel
The chestnut trees
The wishing well

I'll be seeing you
In every lovely summer's day
In everything that's light and gay
I'll always think of you that way

I'll find you in the morning sun
And when the night is new
I'll be looking at the moon
But I'll be seeing you

("I'll be Seeing You," by Sammy Fain and Irving Kahal, 1938)

I will always being seeing you, my dearest Susan, because our love has survived.

Epilogue

It has been almost four years since Susan's death. My journey from the day of her death until now, when I am back on my feet, has not been easy. It wasn't even clear that I would make it. Many people, including my three sons, two stepchildren, and several good friends got me through this ordeal. Five people, in particular, stand out as having provided entirely unexpected advice and assistance that turned out to be extremely helpful for me to eventually become myself again. Once I was through the worst of it, I was in a frame of mind to begin thinking about writing this book, in an effort to further deal with my grief while hopefully giving others the benefit of what Susan and I had experienced together.

Susan was diagnosed with ovarian cancer in May of 2014. As is often the case with ovarian cancer, it was diagnosed at a late stage because there are no tests for it, and symptoms don't occur until later in the disease process, which is why it is so deadly. Of course Susan and I were both devastated. She was only sixty-one. The cancer was all over her pelvis, and the initial treatment was to inject chemo directly into her pelvis to try to kill the cancer at the site. After the treatment, she had a laparoscopic hysterectomy that removed affected organs, and all visible cancer was gone. She did not require further treatment at that time. We were tremendously relieved, but from the wealth of information available online these days, Susan learned her odds for survival were slim because of the late diagnosis. In an effort to take her mind off of the situation, we spent even more time together and began to travel extensively.

About a year and half later, there was evidence of recurrence. I decided to stop trying cases because the preparation and trials were time-consuming, and we wanted to spend as much time together as we could. She began chemotherapy, receiving the medication intravenously once a week for six to eight sessions. She had a phobia about needles and hospitals, so this terrified her. To make matters worse, her veins were not easily accessible, so there was always a problem inserting the IV. She had to take antianxiety medication just to go to the chemo sessions. Each infusion lasted five to six hours because of the different drugs to be administered.

She loved our beach house, so we made a point of spending more time there between sessions. I stopped playing golf so we could have brunch at a new place every Sunday and then take little trips together around the eastern end of Long Island. In 2015 and 2016, we also traveled throughout Europe and the Caribbean, mostly on river or ocean cruises. We spent a lot of time in Paris because that was her favorite city, but we also visited most of Europe's other famous cities, like London, Vienna, Budapest, Prague, Berlin, Nuremberg, Helsinki, Stockholm, Copenhagen, Bergen, Gdańsk, St. Petersburg, Tallinn, and many others. Apparently, the distraction worked because she felt good enough to socialize with strangers. In fact, she met a woman from the Midwest with similar sensibilities, and they hit it off right away, quickly becoming "soul sisters." Even after we returned home, they continued to talk regularly, and Susan was pleased to have made a new friend, even under such dire circumstances. During the winters we went to Arizona because Susan's friends from Minnesota vacationed there. I even arranged chemo sessions at a hospital in Scottsdale to allow us to stay longer.

After about a year, it became apparent that the conventional chemotherapy treatments had not stopped the cancer; she was diagnosed with a pelvic mass. Her doctors at NYU concluded that the tumor was inoperable because of how adherent and intertwined it was to vital organs. Susan was despondent. We left the hospital after learning the news and walked to a restaurant for lunch, but I was determined to show her that all was not lost, so I assured her that I had a plan. I told her I would call an attorney with whom I had tried two cases, who represented Memorial Sloan Kettering, and ask him if he could get us in to see a surgeon for a second opinion. I had not seen this attorney for several years, so you may find this hard to believe, but when we walked into the restaurant immediately after having this conversation, he was sitting right there! To say I was shocked at such an amazing coincidence is an understatement. Leaving Susan at our table, I went over to say hello, then explained our situation and asked for his help. He was happy to help, and later that afternoon we spoke by phone, during which he arranged a conference call with the head of gynecologic surgery, who immediately scheduled a consult for the following day with Sloan's top cancer surgeon.

Sadly, even though we'd been fortunate to receive this second opinion from such an expert, the outcome was the same. The Sloan surgeon concurred that the mass was inoperable and said that even if he were to attempt surgery, Susan would likely not survive because of the damage it would cause her organs. Of course, this all weighed heavily on both of us, and Susan began to tell me her wishes in the event of her death. I took off more time from my law practice to be with her.

Our final option was experimental immunotherapy, but before going down that road there was one more rarely used treatment that was only available if the genetic makeup of the tumor showed she was a viable candidate, which meant a biopsy. They biopsied the pelvic tumor but only got necrotic tissue, which was useless for testing. But her doctors had discovered another mass lower in her pelvis, and I suggested to her surgeon that they biopsy this new tumor. Her surgeon agreed this was a feasible option and did the biopsy.

The weekend after the biopsy, she wasn't feeling well, so on Monday morning we drove to her doctor's. He took some tests and discovered that she had an infection. Her doctor suggested we go to the emergency room where she could be hydrated with fluids and administered antibiotics. After being reassured that she would be transferred to a regular room and continued on IV antibiotics until the infection cleared in a few days, I left her in the hospital on Monday evening. But when I called the next morning to find out what room she had been transferred to, I was told she was in critical care.

I was devastated. I called to tell Lindsay and Danny, and we drove to the hospital together. On the way, her doctor called to tell me to get there as quickly as possible and said he would explain what had happened overnight. When I arrived on Tuesday morning, I was told that she was terminal and that they wanted my approval to discontinue all treatment. Apparently the biopsy had caused an infection in the tumor itself, and because the tumor was inoperable, the infection could not be cured. The infection had caused sepsis, which had spread rapidly, affecting all major organs, so she had "crashed" overnight. Obviously, this came as quite a shock. I asked about the prospect of continuing the antibiotics, but I was told that would only prolong the outcome, not change it. But I couldn't make such an overwhelming decision so quickly, and we agreed to continue the antibiotics to see if there was any positive response.

Within an hour, all my children, her children, and my sister were at her bedside. After an agonizing few hours without any improvement, her children and I agreed to discontinue treatment so she would not suffer, a promise I had made to her. At one point as she lay semi-conscious, I gently shook her. She opened her eyes, and I said, "I love you," which she repeated to me, and we kissed. She closed her eyes. A few hours later, after I had signed the necessary paperwork, I shook her again, but this time she exclaimed, "Phil, stop!" Everyone around the bed broke out laughing. Those were her last words. A friend of mine told me it sounded like she knew what was happening and was telling me she was ready.

The family left by midnight on Tuesday, including her daughter, Lindsay, who could not cope with the situation. Danny and I stayed with her overnight. I got into bed with her, and Susan and I slept together one last time while Danny slept in the chair beside the bed. The next morning, Wednesday, April 5, 2017, while Danny was in the cafeteria and Susan and I were alone, she breathed her last breath at 9:03 AM. She died painlessly and peacefully.

We did not have time to prepare for her death. To describe me as "in despair" doesn't capture the full extent of my depression and dread in the weeks following her death. I have since come to terms with the fact that my suggestion for the second biopsy ultimately resulted in the infection that caused her death. Her surgeon had agreed that it was a good idea, and after all, we had to try every option that could result in a positive outcome. I sought counseling from Will Parker, the therapist I had seen after separating from my second wife, Kathy. He told me I was suffering from post-traumatic stress, as if I had had a physical trauma, except this was emotional. My symptoms were severe depression, recurrent and intrusive recollections of the events in the hospital, and ruminating about carrying her ashes in a tin from the funeral parlor to my house for burial near our home a mere three days after seeing her alive. I also did not want to speak or interact with anyone and had unpredictable and recurrent bouts of crying.

As if that was not enough emotional trauma, I had to come to grips with my own mortality. A few months earlier I had been diagnosed with prostate cancer and had been scheduled for surgery in May. After Susan died, I seriously considered not treating my cancer and dying with her. My sons would receive a healthy sum from my life insurance policies, so in my grief it seemed like a perfectly reasonable solution. My misery would end, and my sons would be taken care of, and that would be that. I told my therapist what I was contemplating. He nodded in understanding and leaned back in his chair, gathering his thoughts for what he was going to say, for which I was totally unprepared. He began by reminding me that I was a successful attorney and obviously had a lot of experience dealing with people and difficult situations throughout my life. He then asked, "Do you think that, with all your life experience, you might have some wisdom to pass on to your grandchildren about how life should be lived and can impart to them lessons you've learned that could be helpful to them in their future?" I was floored.

"Let me think about that one, Will, and I'll get back to you," I answered. Of course that did the trick, and I decided to go through with the prostate surgery.

The first week after Susan's death, I had dinner with an old friend, John Sheehan. Susan had said that she did not want a ceremony, and John and I discussed her wishes. He said that wakes and burials were not for the dead but for the living, to allow them to confront the reality of the death in order to absorb it. He added that Susan wasn't here so she couldn't stop us from having one! I discussed having a shiva with her close cousin Wendy, who thought it was a great idea. When I started to plan it, I realized that all of Susan's family and almost all of her friends were in St. Paul, Minnesota, where she'd grown up, and the last thing she would have wanted was to have my law partners, my friends, and our kids sitting around noshing on food at my apartment in Brooklyn, because her family and friends were in St. Paul and wouldn't be able to come. I decided to have the shiva in St. Paul. Her children, her brother (who lived in Connecticut), and I would go there.

I rented a room in a restaurant and invited fifty of her friends and family. My first words to everyone were that this was something unorthodox that only Susan would appreciate: a shiva in an Italian restaurant! At first, everyone was crying, but by the end we were laughing at the stories we all shared about her. My friend John had been right—this experience helped bring closure to these folks, especially given the suddenness of her passing.

When I returned home from St. Paul, I sought advice from a college friend, Bowen Pak, a math genius and one of the most intelligent people I know. He is religious, so I wanted to know where his faith came from and what he thought about the possibility of a soul existing after death. He explained in a logical way that no one can prove whether there is life after death. Either there is or there isn't, and there's nothing we can do to change that. So if we believe in life after death and discover after we die that we were right, we will be vindicated, but if there is no life after death, we won't be able to do anything to change that anyway. He said, however, if we derive some comfort from believing in life after death—in another realm or dimension—what could be wrong with that? Why not use that belief system as a balm to apply to situations like mine to make our time here a little more palatable? His reasoning about our inability to prove or disprove the existence of life after death is undeniable, and his suggestion to use this fact in a positive way to provide myself some relief from my torment was appealing. His argument lessened much of my pain in dealing with the finality of death, which is one of the hardest things to accept when a loved one dies, especially unexpectedly.

During this time, I also learned something about the Jewish religion that was helpful to me. A few weeks after Susan's death, a Russian Jewish friend of mine, Russell Gladovitser, brought a basket of food and goodies to my house to console me. Russell, who is a loud, boisterous, upbeat man, said in his thick Russian accent, "Phil, you are very lucky man. You have now a guardian angel watching over you and nothing bad will happen to you ever again. Susan watches over you."

"Russell, Jews believe in angels?" I asked.

"Of course!" he bellowed. "From Old Testament." Even though I didn't believe in Catholic angels, let alone Jewish ones, this idea from such an unlikely source gave me solace.

By then I had been fully worked up for my cancer. Everything the doctors told me indicated that they believed my cancer had spread beyond my prostate, because it was an aggressive tumor with a large nodule, suggesting that cells could have escaped the gland. As evidence of how serious they thought the situation was, they detailed the subsequent treatment of radiation and hormone therapy that would be needed if there was evidence of spread, as well as the time involved and the possible, potentially serious complications that could arise from those treatments. They obviously wouldn't have wasted their time or tried to scare me unless they thought that spread was likely. Moreover, the surgery itself was aggressive, because they removed all thirty-seven lymph nodes in my pelvis and seminal vesicles in addition to my prostate. But as it turned out, all the lymph nodes and seminal vesicles were negative for cancer cells, as were all scans of my body after the surgery. For four years now, I have had regular blood tests, and there is no indication of cancer recurrence anywhere. I often think about Russell's words. Just sayin'.

Another person who came out of left field and had a positive effect on me after Susan passed away was someone I hadn't even known when she was alive. About six months after Susan died, I met Hilary Schnitz, a yoga instructor. Twenty years earlier, I had taken a yoga class with Kathy and afterward could barely walk. I never again thought of doing yoga. When I first met Hilary, I told her what I was going through, and she began extolling the benefits of yoga and meditation in dealing with grief. I thought it over and decided to give it a try as a way of doing something Susan and I hadn't done together, to step out on my own and experience things that didn't remind me of her. In one of our early sessions, Hilary also suggested that I take time every week, or however many times I saw fit, to write down three to five things in my life for which I was "grateful." I had never heard of a gratitude journal, but I now know that this practice is used in many therapeutic settings, such as Alcoholics Anonymous. I began doing it after our session each week. Nothing happened right away, but gradually I began to feel a little relief and to appreciate the many positive things and people in my life. I told Will about it, and he remarked that Hilary really knew what she was doing, because it's hard to be depressed and grateful at the same time.

Finally, in January 2018, I had the opportunity to go on a trip to the Far East. I had been invited by Michael Simons, the dean of my law school, St John's, to join him, along with another dean, fifteen students, and some alumni on a trip to China to visit law schools and tour famous sites. During this trip, I met Jack Clark, another alumnus who had come along. We immediately bonded when he told me that he had lost his wife a number of years earlier, and we shared stories about how we had dealt with and were still dealing with our respective losses. It was a relief to hear that I was not crazy and that what I suffered was common. I was also encouraged to hear that he had survived and was now thriving. At some point in the middle of the trip, and without warning, I suddenly felt the weight of the world lifted from my shoulders. I felt like my old self again. I reflected on that and realized that it was probably because I was in a foreign land that I had not visited with Susan and had been thrown in with people I hadn't known beforehand and with whom I was socializing. I was telling jokes, participating in discussions with Chinese law professors, and visiting places that Susan had specifically told me she was not interested in visiting, so there was no connection to her memory. I was doing new things, with new people, making new friends, and it was healing. When I returned home, I felt relieved and more "normal." I sent a note to the dean, explaining my epiphany and thanking him for inviting me.

Of course, I do not want to suggest that I am not sad from time to time or that I don't have difficult days or moments. I talk to Susan every day. She hasn't yet answered me back, but I know exactly what she would say, and that is a comfort. The process I've been through since Susan's death is best articulated by Ethel Person, who wrote, "When love is interrupted by death, the surviving lover may fear the very passage of time that friends look to as balm for the pain. Time may indeed heal, but to the lover time is like a terrible train, rushing the lover away from the last moment with the beloved. Time becomes space and inexorably separates."[148] I have felt both the pain and the healing power of time that Person reflects on with these words.

---

148   Ethel Spector Person, *Dreams of Love and Fateful Encounters: The Power of Romantic Passion* (Ontario, Canada, W.W. Norton, 1988), 57.

As I said in my introduction, this book has been cathartic to write, but it has also been enjoyable because it has helped me recall all that Susan and I had and did in our short ten years together. The week Susan died, I began making random notes about my feelings about what had just happened. That gave me the idea to begin writing about our life together as a way of documenting it and forcing myself to think about and identify what had been so wonderful about what we had. I also started reading about relationships to see how ours compared to others. One book led to another and I discovered that the topics of love and relationships had been written about across vastly different disciplines. I began to see similar threads and concepts in these different approaches and started to summarize and catalog them.

This book is the result of all that research, and it has helped me enormously as I deal with Susan's absence in my life. As others who have written about death have observed, writing about the loss of a loved one is both a testament to that person and a way of keeping them with us. I am incredibly grateful that Susan and I met and had the life we had. I am a better person for it. I hope that our story and my advice here will help others to achieve the same kind of once-in-a-lifetime love that Susan and I had.

Afterword

This book is the result of retrospectively analyzing my relationship with Susan and examining the things we did and didn't do to bring profound change to each of our lives and transform us into a single unit. I dedicated this book to Susan because of the example she set for what it takes to love, how to love, and how to grow in love. She was accomplished in many things, but the model she constructed for how to love is one of her greatest achievements. I have sought to pass on her inspiration and wisdom and what we learned as a couple.

I began my research with the field of psychology, curious to learn what it had to say about love, its origins, and how it figured into relationships. One book led to another and another, in disparate fields, including biology, chemistry, sociology, anthropology, and philosophy, and ultimately to literature, poetry, and music as well. I read more than fifty books covering the subjects and nuances I've written about here and compiled what I thought were the most salient points and compelling analyses to share with readers. I believe I've approached the topic from an entirely different perspective than most who write about and research the complex condition we all know as love. Toward that end, I organized the book according to what I believe is a logical dissection of the topic of love, and I cite experts who have offered useful information on each specific topic.

Some sources are well known and others less so, but I believe all have important viewpoints worth examining.

I also felt it was essential to interweave our story, Susan's and mine, and the methods we used to accomplish what we did. By telling our story, I strove to provide examples in which readers saw themselves and suggestions others could emulate to nurture their own meaningful relationship. I also realized after the fact that writing this book was an integral part of my grieving process and hugely helpful to me.

Writing a book was quite the experience. Budding and experienced writers both are often told to "write about what you know." What I know is my love for Susan and her love for me, and I hope this book expresses that in a way that has a broad and meaningful impact.

About the Author

What qualifies me to write an advice book about love? Fair question. The answer is twofold: first, the strength of my relationship with Susan and the knowledge I gained through it; and second, the exhaustive research I conducted into the many scientific dimensions of love and relationships.

Additionally, I have spent forty-five years as a trial lawyer, where I have learned how to successfully manage relationships with all types of people, from colleagues to adversaries, judges, and clients, and often in the difficult circumstances of litigation. Moreover, running a law firm with a wide spectrum of personalities has gifted me insight into how to create and maintain a harmonious atmosphere. My extensive law-practice and law firm–management work has also honed my emotional intelligence, a crucial component of effective relationships.

I also discovered that my analytical, organizational, and research skills, developed in medical malpractice cases for over thirty-five years, were a huge plus in helping me write a book that brought so many disciplines together to focus on a single topic.

Finally, the experiences in my prior marriages, both positive and negative, and what I learned in therapy about them and myself, also substantially advanced my knowledge in this area. I was married twice before Susan. Mary and I were married for twenty years, and she is the mother of my three grown children. Kathy and I were married for six years and had been together for four years before marriage.

The breakup of my second marriage led me to therapy to dissect and assess the role I had played in the failure of both relationships. I learned a great deal about myself, becoming more sensitive and in touch with my emotions, though I've no doubt that both Mary and Kathy will howl with laughter at the notion. But in truth, therapy was an eye-opening experience and prepared me for entering a new relationship on stronger footing and with greater sensitivity. In a real sense, the relationships with my first two wives (each different from each other and my relationship with Susan) gave me more acute awareness of issues as they arose, allowing me to address them more positively than I had done in the past.

Today I have excellent relationships with both former wives. I often speak to and see my first wife, Mary, especially as we co-grandparent our four grandchildren. We have been on family vacations together with our children and grandchildren. Kathy and I were divorced almost twenty years ago, and we remain colleagues at my law firm.

I'd like to thank both Mary and Kathy for being forgiving and understanding as they read this book (assuming they do read it!). I believe, as I hope they do, that we each did the best we could at the time. I'm pleased that we continue to remain friends, and I am eternally grateful for how those experiences taught me lessons I brought to my marriage with Susan and made their way into this book.

Don'ts and Dos:
Your Road Map to a
Lifetime of Love

(Please feel free to tear or cut out this helpful reminder.)

DON'T

1. Ever raise your voice at your partner.

2. Ever call your partner a name (other than the pet name(s) you have for each other).

3. Criticize, condemn, or complain to your partner about something they do, especially in front of others.

4. Tell your partner what to do about their own issues, unless asked.

DO

1. Things for the other person without being asked.

2. Talk to each other in person at least once a day and for at least thirty minutes, without any distractions.

3. Always respect the other person. This means loving them for who they are and not for who you want them to be.

4. Participate in activities together.

5. Make an effort with your appearance and grooming habits to show that you care what your mate thinks of you.

6. Give your partner the space they need to be/do their own thing.

Acknowledgments

This book could not have been possible without the specific contributions of each of the people who helped me along the way. First, there was the editorial prowess of Lisa Messinger. It was her skill with the English language and her patience in dealing with me that allowed this book to happen. I had ideas and wrote from the heart. She made sure it was understandable and that I didn't get bogged down in so much detail that it became incomprehensible. In the process of sharing all this personal information, we became good friends. Thank you, Lisa.

Melanie Votow made further edits that made the book "publishable" and oversaw the book-proposal process that presented it in its best light. She also introduced me to Mike Coffino, another friend I made in this process. He provided the positive feedback, which kept me encouraged to continue attempting to get this published after so many others declined. He also suggested the finishing touches that softened the rough edges and made suggestions that resulted in the inclusion of poignant love stories, other than my own, to which the reader could relate, which reflected the validity of my recommendations.

Another integral person was Stacey Crew. She shepherded the book through the final stages of actually getting it published. She was invaluable in understanding and overseeing everything that needed to be done to have a product that could come to market. She coordinated the social media team, with the publisher, and made sure every detail that had to be done got done correctly and on time. Thank you, Stacey.

There was an entire social media/marketing/website creation aspect of this process that was new to me, and it was Susan Sipe and her crew of Ronnie Gee and Adam Vargas who were able to put it all together in the most professional and efficient manner.

Finally, special thanks to John Koehler who believed in the message of this book and had the confidence in it to publish it. Thank you, John.

Bibliography

Ackerman, J. M., Griskevicius, V., and Li, N. P., "Let's get serious: communicating commitment in romantic relationships," *Journal of Personality and Social Psychology*, 100 (2011): 1079-1094.

Berridge, Kent C., "Comparing the Emotional Brains of Humans and Other Animals," *Handbook of Affective Sciences*, ed. R. J. Davison, K. R. Scherer, and H. H. Goldsmith, New York, Oxford University Press, 2003): 25-51.

Brown, Asa Don, "Please Yell at Me: The effects of yelling and verbal abuse," *Psychology Today*, (Apr 21, 2017).

Buscaglia, Leo, *Love: What Life is All About*, (New York: Random House Publishing Group, 1972).

Buss, D. M., "Sex differences in human mate preferences: Evolutionary hypotheses tested in 37 cultures," *Behavioral & Brain Sciences*, 12 (1989) 1-49.

Buss, David M. & Schmitt, David P., "Sexual Strategies Theory: An evolutionary perspective on human mating," *Psychological Review*, 100 (1993): 204-232.

Buss, D. M., *Evolutionary Psychology: The New Science of the Mind*, (Boston: Pearson, 2008).

Carter, Rita, *Mapping the Mind*, (Oakland, CA, University of CA Press, 2010).

Damasio, Antonio, *Looking for Spinoza: Joy, Sorrow and the Feeling Brain*, (New York: Harcourt Brace, 2003).

Damasio, Antonio, "A Second Chance for Emotion," *Cognitive Neuroscience of Emotion*, ed. Richard Lane and Lynn Nadel, (New York: Oxford Univ. Press, 2000).

DelPriore, D. J., Prokosch, M. L., & Hill, S. E., "The causes and consequences of women's competitive beautification," ed. Maryanne L. Fisher, *The Oxford Handbook of Women and Competition*, (New York: Oxford Univ. Press, 2017).

Devoldre, I., Davis M. H., Verofstadt, L. L., Buysse A., "Empathy and social support provision in couples: social support and the need to study the underlying processes," *Journal of Psychology Interdisciplinary and Applied*, (2010): 144, 259-284.

DiDonato, Theresa, "Who Says Those 3 Words First (and Why It Matters)," *Psychology Today*, (Mar 24, 2016).

Dungan, Nathan, *Money Sanity Solutions*, (Minneapolis: Share Save Spend, 2010).

Ekman, Paul, "An argument for basic emotions," *Cognition and Emotions*, Vol 6:3-4 (1992).

Erwin, Philip G., Burke, Annie, Purves, David G., "Food Sharing and Perceptions of the Status of a Relationship," *Perceptual & Motor Skills*, (2002).

Felmlee, Diane H, Sprecher, Susan, *The Handbook of the Sociology of Emotions*, Vol. II, ed. Jan E. Stets and Jonathan H. Turner, (New York: Springer Science & Business Media, LLC, 2006).

Fisher, Helen, *Anatomy of Love: A Natural History of Mating, Marriage, and Why We Stray*, (New York: W.W. Norton & Company, Inc., 2016).

Fisher, Maryanne L., Garcia, Justin R., Sokol Chang, Rosemarie, Editors, *Evolution's Empress, Darwinian Perspectives on the Nature of Women*, (New York, Oxford Univ. Press, 2013).

Fisher, Maryanne L., Editor, *The Oxford Handbook of Women and Competition*, (New York: Oxford Univ. Press, 2017).

Fisher, Maryanne, Costello, Victoria, *The Complete Idiot's Guide to the Chemistry of Love* (New York: Penguin Group, 2010).

Franks, David, *The Handbook of the Sociology of Emotions*, Vol. II, ed. Jan E. Stets and Jonathan H. Turner, (New York: Springer Science & Business Media, LLC, 2006).

Fredrickson, Barbara, L., *Love 2.0, How Our Supreme Emotion Affects Everything We Feel, Think, Do and Become*, (New York: Penguin Group, 2013).

Fromm, Erich, *The Art of Loving*, (New York: Harper & Row, Inc., 1956).

Gates, Melinda, *The Moment of Lift: How Empowering Women Changes the World*, (New York: Flatiron Books, 2019).

Gazzaniga, Michael S., *The Mind's Past*, (Oakland, CA: University of California Press, 1998).

Gordon, Sherri, "9 Consequences of Name-Calling," *verywellfamily. com*, (Sept. 2019).

Gottman, John, *Why Marriages Succeed or Fail, and How You Can Make Yours Last,* (New York: Simon & Schuster, 1994).

Gottman, John, *The Seven Principles for Making Marriage Work,* (New York, Harmony Books, 2015).

Guëguen, Nicolas, "Bust size and hitchhiking: a field study," *Perceptual and Motor Skills* 105 (3 Pt 2) (January 2008): 1294-1298.

Guëguen, Nicolas, "Women's bust size and men's courtship solicitation," *Body Image* 4(4) (January 2008): 386-390.

Hamburg, Myrte E., Finkenauer, Catrin, and Schuengel, Carlo, "Food for love: the role of food offering in empathic emotion regulation," *Frontiers in Psychology*, 5:32, 2014.

Harrison, M. A., & Shortall, J. C., "Women and men in love: who really feels it and says it first?" *The Journal of Social Psychology*, (2011): 151, 727-736.

Hendrix, Harville, *Getting the Love You Want: A Guide for Couples,* (New York: Henry Holt and Co., 1988).

Hendrix, Harville, Hunt, Helen LaKelly, *Keeping the Love You Find: A Guide for Singles,* (New York: Atria Books, 1992).

hooks, bell, *All About Love,* (New York: HarperCollins, 2000).

Izard, Carroll, *The Psychology of Emotions,* (New York: Plenum Press, 1991).

Johnsen, Laurel L., Geher, Glenn, "Fashion as a Set of Signals in Female Intrasexual Competition," ed. Maryanne Fisher, *The Oxford Handbook of Women and Competition,* (New York: Oxford Univ. Press, 2017).

Jones, Martin, *Feast: Why Humans Share Food,* (Oxford: Oxford University Press, 2007).

Kalmijn, Matthijis, "Intermarriage and Homogamy: Causes, Patterns, Trends," *Annual Review of Sociology,* 24 (1998): 395-421.

Lakoff, George, and Mark Johnson, *Philosophy in the Flesh: The Embodied Mind and its Challenge to Western Thought,* (New York: Basic Books, 1999).

LeDoux, Joseph, "Cognitive–Emotional Interactions: Listen to the Brain," *Cognitive Neuroscience of Emotion,* ed. Richard Lane and Lynn Nadel, (New York: Oxford University Press, 2000): 129-155.

LeDoux, Joseph, *The Emotional Brain, The Mysterious Underpinnings of Emotional Life,* (New York: Simon & Schuster, 1996).

Lerner, Harriet, *Marriage Rules: A Manual for the Married and Coupled Up,* (New York: Penguin Random House, 2012).

Leung, Wency, "Love and Food Have Always Been Intertwined," *The Globe and Mail Newspaper,* (Toronto, ON, Canada, Feb. 2012).

Lewis, Thomas, Amini, Fari, Lannon, Richard, *A General Theory of Love,* (New York: Random House, 2000).

Libet, Benjamin, "Neural Time Factors in Conscious and Unconscious Mental Functions," *Toward a Science of Consciousness, First Discussion and Debates,* ed. R. Hameroff, A.W. Kaszniak, and A. Scott, (Cambridge MA, MIT Press, 1996): 337-347.

Massey, Douglas S., "A Brief History of Human Society: The Origin and Role of Emotion in Social Life," *American Sociological Review,* 67: pp. 1-29, 2002.

Merton, Thomas, *Love and Living,* ed. Naomi Burton Stone and Brother Patrick Hart, (New York: Farrar, Straus and Giroux, 1979).

Miller, Lisa, Rozin, Paul, & Fiske, Alan P., "Food sharing and feeding another person suggest intimacy: Two studies of American college students," *European Journal of Social Psychology*, 28(3) (1998): 423-436.

Mitchell, Stephen A., *Can Love Last, The Fate of Romance Over Time* (New York: W.W. Norton & Company, 2002).

Morris, P., White, J., Morrison E., and Fisher, K., "High heels as supernormal stimuli: How wearing high heels affects judgements of female attractiveness," *Evolution and Human Behavior*, 34 (2013): 176-181.

Nouwen, Henri J. M., *The Inner Voice of Love: A Journey Through Anguish to Freedom*, (Danvers, MA: Image Books, 1999).

Ortigue, Stephanie, Bianchi-Demichelli, Francesco, Patel, Nisa, Frum, Chris, and James, Lewis W., "Neuroimaging of Love: fMRI Meta-Analysis Evidence Toward New Perspectives in Sexual Medicine," *Journal of Sexual Medicine*, 7 (2010): 3541-3552.

Pawelski, Suzann and James O., *Happy Together: Using the Science of Positive Psychology to Build Love That Lasts*, (New York: Penguin Random House, 2018).

Peck, M. Scott, *The Road Less Traveled: A New Psychology of Love, Traditional Values and Spiritual Growth*, (New York: Touchstone, 1978).

Person, Ethel Spector, *Dreams of Love and Fateful Encounters: The Power of Romantic Passion*, (Ontario, Canada: W.W. Norton, 1988).

Pogue, David, "Your Best Tips for Managing the Family Money," (quoting Susan Winslow), *New York Times*, June 26, 2019.

Primoff, Walter, "Your Best Tips for Managing the Family Money," *New York Times*, June 26, 2019.

Sobal, Jeffery, Bove, Caron F., Rauschenbach, Barbara S., "Commensal careers at entry into marriage: establishing commensal units and managing commensal circles," *Sociological Review,* 50 (2008): 378-397.

Stets, Jan E. and Turner, Jonathan H., Editors, *The Handbook of the Sociology of Emotions,* (New York: Springer Science & Business Media, LLC, 2006).

Tillotson, Giles, *Taj Mahal* (Wonders of the World), (Cambridge, MA: Harvard University Press, 2008).

Trillin, Calvin, *About Alice,* (New York: Random House, 2006).

Walters, Sally and Crawford, Charles B., "The Importance of Mate Attraction for Intrasexual Competition in Men and Women," *Ethology and Sociobiology,* 15(1) (1994): 5-30.

Wilkerson, Isabel, *Caste: The Origins of Our Discontents*, (New York: Random House, 2020).